BASICS

MARKETING

01

Hayden Noel

Consumer behaviour

Ethical: aware-
ness/
reflect-
ion/
debate

ava
academia

An AVA Book

Published by AVA Publishing SA

Rue des Fontenailles 16
Case Postale
1000 Lausanne 6
Switzerland

Tel: +41 786 005 109
Email: enquiries@avabooks.ch

Distributed by Thames & Hudson (ex-North America)

181a High Holborn
London WC1V 7QX
United Kingdom

Tel: +44 20 7845 5000
Fax: +44 20 7845 5055
Email: sales@thameshudson.co.uk
www.thamesandhudson.com

Distributed in the USA & Canada by:
Ingram Publisher Services Inc.

1 Ingram Blvd.
La Vergne, TN 37086
USA

Tel: +1 866 400 5351
Fax: +1 800 838 1149
Email: customer.service@ingrampublisherservices.com

English Language Support Office

AVA Publishing (UK) Ltd.
Tel: +44 1903 204 455
Email: enquiries@avabooks.ch

Copyright © AVA Publishing SA 2009

ISBN 978-2-940373-84-0

10 9 8 7 6 5 4 3 2 1

Design by David Shaw

Production by AVA Book Production Pte. Ltd., Singapore

Tel: +65 6334 8173
Fax: +65 6259 9830
Email: production@avabooks.com.sg

Carfun footprint – MINI advert
As consumers become more concerned with fuel consumption, for reasons of both economy and ecology, many car companies have begun to use fuel economy as a key selling feature (see pp. 124–129).

DRIVE LIKE THERE IS A TOMORROW.

The 37-mile-per-gallon*MINI Cooper has the best Carfun Footprint™ on the road. Designed around our philosophy of MINIMALISM, every MINI maximizes your driving fun while minimizing your environmental impact. Calculate your Carfun Footprint and see where your vehicle stacks up at **CarfunFootprint.com**

MINI COOPER

CARFUN FOOTPRINT .COM

Table of contents

✕

Coca-Cola – a category exempla

If you are selling a generic product it can be beneficial to model your labelling and packaging on the best-known brand in that market – also known as category exemplar or prototype. In the soft drinks market that would be Coca-Cola (see pp. 112–113).

Introduction
> How to get the most out of this book

The study of consumer behaviour touches almost every aspect of our lives. From the time we wake up, brush our teeth (probably using the same Colgate toothpaste that our parents used when we were growing up) and eat a breakfast of our favourite Kellogg's cereal; until we go to sleep setting the alarm on our Sony radio.

We spend much of our waking day being consumers and many of our everyday actions are part of the study of consumer behaviour, such as:

- how we perceive advertising
- how our attitudes are formed
- how we make decisions and what factors influence these decisions
- how we use and dispose of products and services.

These actions collectively make us part of a consumer society and much of the meaning in our society is derived from our actions as either buyers or sellers. Therefore, the study of consumer behaviour can help us understand the business of marketing and can also result in us being better-informed consumers.

Currently there are two general approaches to the study of consumer behaviour: a micro approach that examines the consumer as an individual and studies the many psychological and other processes that consumers use when they acquire, consume and dispose of goods and services; and a macro approach that focuses on how the consumer functions within a group setting and how this influences their behaviour.

This book flows from a macro orientation in the earlier chapters to a micro orientation in the latter chapters. The early chapters rely on theories from sociology and anthropology whereas the latter chapters draw heavily from the study of psychology. This approach will allow you to understand the consumer as an individual and also better understand the consumer's role within society. These chapters all fit within a broad conceptual model that provides a 'big picture' framework to help enhance your understanding of the material.

The digital age has resulted in the shrinking of borders and a wider marketplace for consumers. It is almost as easy for a consumer in Taiwan to purchase a CD from a vendor in Taipei as it is for her to purchase one from a vendor in Sydney, Australia. This book considers the many different consumers around the world and explores how their behaviour differs. There are many examples of consumers and companies in different countries around the globe, producing a borderless marketplace that is heavily influenced by the worldwide digital explosion.

Chapter 1
What is consumer behaviour?

Chapter 1 provides an introduction to the study of consumer behaviour and sets the tone for the rest of the book. It illustrates the breadth of consumer behaviour and highlights the many ways in which it touches our lives. It also examines the structural framework that can be used to understand the different interrelationships between the concepts presented in the rest of the book. The latter part of this chapter examines the process of consumer research and its related techniques.

Chapter 2
Ethnic, religious and group influences

Chapter 2 examines how ethnic and religious influences affect consumer behaviour. The chapter concludes with a discussion of how the reference groups to which we belong (such as our colleagues and friends) can influence the way in which we acquire, use and dispose of goods and services.

Chapter 3
Class, age and gender influences

Chapter 3 explores how social class is determined and how social factors such as class, age and gender can influence consumers' actions.

Chapter 4
Consumer motivation, perception and attitude

Chapter 4 presents an in depth review of consumer needs and motivations, by examining the cognitive (thinking), affective (feeling) and conative (doing) bases of consumer action. In addition, it covers the impact of consumer perception and consumer attitudes on marketing strategy.

Chapter 5
Consumer knowledge and memory

Chapter 5 examines how consumers interpret new stimuli using their existing knowledge, and how they try to understand this new information. In addition, since existing information stored in a consumer's memory is often used to aid in making choices, this chapter also explores how memories are formed, stored and retrieved.

Chapter 6
The consumer as a decision maker

The final chapter investigates the sequential process of consumer decision making – problem recognition, information search, evaluation, choice and post-decision processes.

Basics Marketing: Consumer behaviour offers students an accessible and visually engaging introduction to the study and understanding of why people behave as they do. It also demonstrates how this knowledge can lead to the development of more effective marketing plans. Key concepts and theories are clearly explained and reinforced with real-world examples in the case studies, while end-of-chapter discussion questions and student exercises help to further develop the concepts learned in each section.

Case studies offer insight into the working methods of some of the world's most interesting campaigns.

Discussion questions and exercises consolidate and contextualise the key points covered in each chapter.

Images and captions illustrate key concepts, behaviour and campaigns.

Chapter navigation highlights the current chapter unit and lists the previous and following sections.

Thinking points put the ideas discussed in the main text in a real-world context.

Quotations help to place the topic being discussed into context.

Running glossary provides the definitions of key terms highlighted in the main text.

< Consumer-related reference groups
Case study / McDonald's goes global
>Questions and exercises

62/ 63

The impact of religion on McDonald's operations

In addition to cultural norms, another major factor that impacts on the company's marketing strategy is the religion of the customer base. For example, all McDonald's restaurants in Israel serve kosher food. However, although there are over 100 McDonald's restaurants in Israel only a dozen or so are strictly kosher since they do not serve dairy and are closed on the Sabbath. In addition, McDonald's has restaurants that serve halal food. Like kosher-prepared meals, halal meals must be prepared in accordance with the relevant religious principles. In April 2007, McDonald's opened its first restaurant in London that served halal food. These attempts to satisfy religious norms have met with success; the halal restaurant in London has had visitors from all over Europe.[15]

Question 1
Does McDonald's have an appropriate global marketing strategy? What, if anything, should they change?

Question 2
Do you believe that McDonald's responds to religious influences appropriately?

Question 3
In what other ways, in addition to restaurant design and the food, could McDonald's respond to the different cultural/religious influences of the countries in which it operates?

Unusual neighbours
A McDonald's drive-thru sign sits somewhat incongruously next to a temple in Bangkok, Thailand. McDonald's has achieved global success by making small but significant concessions to the different cultures of the countries where it establishes restaurants (for example, in line with local tastes, McThai serves several fish and chicken dishes but has fewer beef options).

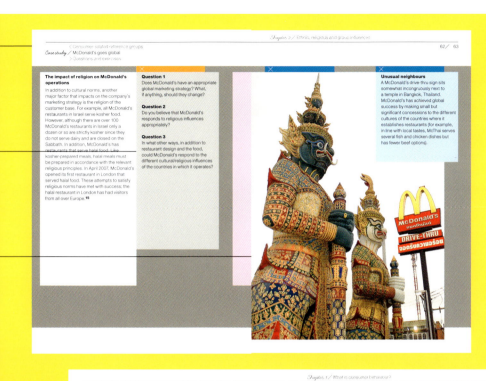

Defining consumer behaviour
>What influences consumer behaviour?

The study of consumer behaviour examines the **products** and services consumers buy and use and how these purchases influence their daily lives. This field covers a lot of ground. It has been defined as: 'the study of the processes involved when consumers acquire, consume and dispose of goods, services, activities, ideas in order to satisfy their needs and desires'.[3] This definition has some very important elements, which we will examine more closely.

Who is the consumer?
We usually think of the consumer as the person who identifies a need or desire, searches for a product to satisfy this need, buys the product and then consumes the product in order to satisfy the need. However, in many cases, different individuals may be involved in this chain of events. For instance, in the case of a laptop the purchaser may be a parent and the user a teenage son or daughter. Companies must account for all of the different individuals involved in the acquisition and consumption process.

It is also important to note that the study of consumer behaviour is not limited to how a person purchases tangible products such as a bottle of water or a new camera. Consumer behaviour also examines the acquisition of services such as a contract for a broadband Internet service. It also includes how consumers pursue activities such as attending a gym or booking a holiday.

Consumer behaviour and buying
Consumer behaviour examines how individuals acquire, use and dispose of company offerings. Goods and services can be acquired through purchase, but they can also be obtained through **barter**, **leasing** or borrowing. After consumers acquire an item, they then use it in some manner. This could mean that the offering is consumed in one use (for example, a can of Coca-Cola), or it could be consumed over time (such as a mobile phone). Usage could also influence the behaviour of others.

If a product performs well then satisfied consumers can encourage others to adopt it through positive reviews; on the other hand, dissatisfied consumers can complain and encourage behaviour ranging from non-purchase of a product to boycotting a company's entire product line. Lastly, consumer behaviour includes what occurs after a product is used. For example, some companies spend a great deal of money to create products that can be recycled in some way. Consumers who are concerned about the environment identify with these companies and are more likely to purchase their products and services.

Being Frank
In this chapter we will examine the different domains of the study of consumer behaviour. To help put the ideas into context we will use a hypothetical iPhone customer named Frank.

Frank is a 22-year-old college student; he works part-time, but is a full-time student. Like most iPhone consumers, he is open-minded and likes to try new things. He tends to adopt new products fairly early in their life cycle. However, like most young consumers who are not employed full-time, he is not always able to afford the high-tech products he craves.

Running glossary
barter
exchange (goods or services) for other goods or services

leasing
describes a contract by which one party conveys land, property or services to another (for a specified time) in return for payment

product
an article or substance manufactured for sale

It used to be that people needed products to survive. Now products need people to survive.
Nicholas Johnson

On 29 June 2007 Apple launched the iPhone in the US amid much fanfare about its touch screen interface, Internet capability and iPod features.[1] In spite of its hefty price tag ($499–$599) 170,000 iPhones were sold in the first two days and sales topped one million units by September 2007. However, Apple received hundreds of complaints from early iPhone purchasers when the company reduced the price by $200 two months after the launch. Apple responded immediately with $100 store credit to any Apple store or the Apple website.[2]

The launch of the iPhone illustrates some of the questions that can be answered through the study of consumer behaviour. Which consumer needs were met by the iPhone? What motivated consumers to line up for days outside of Apple and AT&T stores to ensure that they were able to purchase the phone? Why was the phone so successful? Why did consumers react so negatively to the drop in price? Why did Apple react by offering iPhone owners $100 worth of credit? Finding answers to these questions and understanding why consumers behave the way they do is critical to any firm's success.

Apple's iPhone

Hundreds of people lined up – some for up to five days – outside Apple stores and outlets of AT&T for the launch of Apple's much-hyped iPhone.

The study of consumer behaviour examines the **product**s and services consumers buy and use and how these purchases influence their daily lives. This field covers a lot of ground. It has been defined as: 'the study of the processes involved when consumers acquire, consume and dispose of goods, services, activities, ideas in order to satisfy their needs and desires'.[3] This definition has some very important elements, which we will examine more closely.

Who is the consumer?

We usually think of the consumer as the person who identifies a need or desire, searches for a product to satisfy this need, buys the product and then consumes the product in order to satisfy the need. However, in many cases, different individuals may be involved in this chain of events. For instance, in the case of a laptop the purchaser may be a parent and the user a teenage son or daughter. Companies must account for all of the different individuals involved in the acquisition and consumption process.

It is also important to note that the study of consumer behaviour is not limited to how a person purchases tangible products such as a bottle of water or a new camera. Consumer behaviour also examines the acquisition of services such as a contract for a broadband Internet service. It also includes how consumers pursue activities such as attending a gym or booking a holiday.

Running glossary

barter
exchange (goods or services) for other goods or services

leasing
describes a contract by which one party conveys land, property or services to another (for a specified time) in return for payment

product
an article or substance manufactured for sale

It used to be that people needed products to survive. Now products need people to survive.
Nicholas Johnson

Consumer behaviour and buying

Consumer behaviour examines how individuals acquire, use and dispose of company offerings. Goods and services can be acquired through purchase, but they can also be obtained through **barter**, **leasing** or borrowing. After consumers acquire an item, they then use it in some manner. This could mean that the offering is consumed in one use (for example, a can of Coca-Cola), or it could be consumed over time (such as a mobile phone). Usage could also influence the behaviour of others.

If a product performs well then satisfied consumers can encourage others to adopt it through positive reviews; on the other hand, dissatisfied consumers can complain and encourage behaviour ranging from non-purchase of a product to boycotting a company's entire product line. Lastly, consumer behaviour includes what occurs after a product is used. For example, some companies spend a great deal of money to create products that can be recycled in some way. Consumers who are concerned about the environment identify with these companies and are more likely to purchase their products and services.

Being Frank

In this chapter we will examine the different domains of the study of consumer behaviour. To help put the ideas into context we will use a hypothetical iPhone customer named Frank.

Frank is a 22-year-old college student; he works part-time, but is a full-time student. Like most iPhone consumers, he is open-minded and likes to try new things. He tends to adopt new products fairly early in their life cycle. However, like most young consumers who are not employed full-time, he is not always able to afford the high-tech products that he craves.

As consumers go through their day, buying, using and disposing of companies' offerings, what are the various factors that impact on their decisions? What forces are operating to lead them to purchase the product and brand that they finally choose? There are several factors that can impact on consumer behaviour. These factors can be grouped into three conceptual domains:

■ external influences
■ internal processes (including consumer decision making)
■ post-decision processes.

These three groups will also serve as the framework for this book. For the purposes of conceptual clarity, each area is discussed separately in the text but in reality they are interrelated. External influences, such as a consumer's **culture**, have a direct impact on the internal, psychological processes and other factors that lead to different consumer decisions being made. For instance, a consumer's religion could impact on their attitudes towards eating beef or other types of meat; or their age could impact on their ability to **perceive** fast-moving objects in certain television commercials.

Running glossary

culture
the ideas, customs and social behaviour of a particular people or society

perceive
be aware or conscious of (something); come to realise or understand

The model of consumer behaviour
The diagram opposite illustrates the various influences and processes that affect an individual consumer's decisions. The three major factors are: external influences (such as the individual's cultural background), internal processes (such as the individual's reason for making the purchase) and post-decision processes (did the product live up to the consumer's expectations?).[4]

The model of consumer behaviour

External influences

Firm's marketing efforts
Product
Promotion
Price
Place

The consumer's culture
Religion
Ethnicity
Reference groups
Social class

Internal processes

Psychological processes
Motivation
Perception
Attitudes
Knowledge

Decision making
Problem recognition
Information search
Judgment
Decision making

Post-decision processes

Purchase
Post-purchase behaviour

〈 Defining consumer behaviour
What influences consumer behaviour?
〉 Consumers' impact on marketing strategy

External influences

External influences focus on the various factors that impact upon consumers as they identify which needs to satisfy and which products and services to use to satisfy those needs. These forces fall into two major categories: the efforts of the firm; and the various factors that make up the consumer's culture. The marketing efforts of the firm include the product being offered for sale, its price, the places it's offered for sale, and how they choose to promote it. These forces are fairly uniform, regardless of the individual needs and background of the consumer. In Chapters 2 and 3 we will be concentrating on the other external factors, which lie in the domain of consumer behaviour.

Culture is a shared, learned, symbolic system of values, beliefs and attitudes that shapes and influences perception and behaviour – an abstract 'mental blueprint' or 'code'. It leads to a set of expected behaviours and **norm**s for a specific group of people. As the definition suggests, culture has a tremendous impact on many aspects of human behaviour. Consumers have certain attitudes, and value certain objects because of the unique system of beliefs that define the group to which they belong. Additionally, culture can influence how we perceive and eventually process information. Let's use Frank and his iPhone to illustrate how the different domains could impact upon consumer behaviour.

Religious and ethnic influences

Religion provides individuals with a structured set of beliefs and values that guide their behaviour and help them make choices. Some religious groups, such as the Amish in the United States, do not believe in using modern technology. In the case of the iPhone, Frank decides to camp out in front of an Apple store in Chicago in order to be one of the first in line to purchase the device. His behaviour would not be typical of an Amish teenager.

Age and new technology

Marketers are very aware that the age of the consumer is important when determining who will try a new product or service. This is especially true for products that are based on recently developed technology. For example, even though ownership of MP3 players increased by 150% from December 2003 to December 2008, younger consumers are still much more likely to own one of these devices. Children aged between 12 and 17 years old are 2.5 times more likely to own an MP3 player than all other consumers.[5]

Age and gender

Many young men in Frank's age group tend to be innovators. They take risks and are very willing to try new products and ideas. A novel product such as the iPhone would not intimidate them in any way. Conversely, many older consumers, who might not be as technologically savvy, may be reluctant to spend $500/£350 on such a device.

The use of new technology by younger consumers is also evident in the development of on-demand television. Many consumers no longer watch shows at the time they are initially run; instead they take advantage of technologies which let them view their favourite shows long after they have been shown, such as digital video recorders, the Internet, Video on Demand and MP3 players that can show high-resolution movies. Younger consumers have adopted these new television options at a much faster rate than their older counterparts. A study conducted by the Nielsen Group in 2007 found that 56% of 18–34-year-old adults use these new technologies compared to 21% for viewers aged over 55.[6]

Reference groups

A reference group is a set of people with whom individual consumers compare themselves in developing their own attitudes and behaviour. Reference groups have a significant impact on consumption of products and services. They convey information to an individual about which products and services they should or should not be consuming.

This is especially true for individuals who consider themselves to be very similar to their peers or reference groups. Frank perceives himself as being very similar to his fellow college students. The majority of college students want to be viewed as trendy and stylish; for them the cachet of the iPhone is very difficult to resist. Therefore, Frank is highly motivated to wait in line for many hours in order to obtain his own iPhone.

Social class

The concept of social class implies that some people have more power, wealth and opportunity than others. Some consumers try to indicate which social class they belong to by consuming certain products and services. For example, they may engage in conspicuous consumption or may use products that indicate a certain status. Given the relatively high price of the iPhone, the average iPhone buyer would most likely belong to the middle or upper social class.

Running glossary

norm
a standard or pattern, especially of social behaviour, that is typical or expected

〈 Defining consumer behaviour
What influences consumer behaviour?
〉 Consumers' impact on marketing strategy

Internal processes

Internal processes are the psychological factors inherent in each individual. In Chapters 4, 5 and 6 we'll see in detail how motivation, attitudes and decision making all work together with the external factors described previously to influence consumers' decision making and purchases.

Motivation

Motivation has been defined as an 'inner state of arousal' with the resulting energy being directed towards achieving a goal.[7] The goal in Frank's case is obtaining the iPhone. Apple engaged in an extensive promotion strategy months before the official launch of the iPhone. This led to consumers becoming energised, ready and willing to engage in behaviour that would lead to acquiring the iPhone. In the US, in order to use the iPhone these consumers needed to sign a two-year contract with AT&T. This made the decision a risky one – purchasing the phone involved a significant time commitment. In addition, a significant cash investment was necessary. Given both the financial and time risk, Frank is highly motivated to learn about the various alternatives available to him and also to learn about all of the iPhone options before he makes the purchase.

Running glossary

categorisation
place in a particular class or group

stimuli
a thing that arouses activity or energy in someone or something; a spur or incentive

Selective perception

Consumers are exposed to multiple marketing **stimuli** every day in the form of advertising and promotions. Since the brain's capacity to process information is limited, consumers tend to be very selective about what they pay attention to. When planning to purchase a product, given the many options displayed in various media, consumers cannot attend to all of the products being advertised and must engage in selective perception. Thus they only pay attention to the few items that would fit their needs.[8]

Perception

Since Frank is highly motivated to make the iPhone purchase, he makes sure that he is exposed to and pays attention to information related to the phone. He notices ads for the phone and pays attention to any facts stated in those ads. The iPhone faces competition from several manufacturers who offer competing products. Since Frank is inundated with information about different types of phones, he only pays selective attention to iPhone advertisements. He attends to information about the iPhone that will enable him to make an informed purchase decision.

Knowledge

In this context, knowledge reflects the information an individual gathers about different brands, companies, product categories, how to buy products and also how to use products. Consumers often organise this knowledge into categories of similar objects. This process of **categorisation** helps consumers quickly assess the possible uses for particular products. Frank uses the knowledge that he gathers, and tries to categorise and comprehend it. For instance, he might categorise the iPhone as a new type of personal digital assistant that comes with an MP3 player and phone. This enables him to fully understand the capabilities of the new phone.

An idea can turn to dust or magic depending on the talent that rubs against it.
William Bernbach

Attitudes

Attitudes do not always predict behaviour. For example, many consumers may have a positive attitude towards the iPhone, but this positivity may not necessarily result in their making a purchase. Additionally, consumer attitudes may change over time and as they gain access to additional information. For example, as Frank is exposed to new information, his evaluation of the iPhone might change. A positive review from a publication like *Which?* or *Consumer Reports* that publishes independent, scientifically conducted reviews about numerous products and services may lead him to shift his evaluation upward. This positive attitude would mean that he would be more likely to purchase the phone.

Consumer awareness shifts attitudes

Hybrid cars, such as the Toyota Prius, feature a small fuel-efficient engine combined with an electric motor that assists the engine when accelerating. Sales of these cars have increased over the past few years as attitudes towards the environment have shifted. As consumers learn more about the impact of automobile emissions on the environment, more individuals are considering purchasing environmentally friendly vehicles. An increased awareness about global warming and other environmental issues have caused a shift in consumer attitudes and behaviour. Manufacturers and marketers ignore such shifts at their peril.

Memory

Consumer memory is a great store of knowledge that people have acquired over time. Memory holds information about products, services, shopping and product usage experiences. Retrieval is the act of remembering the information that we have stored in memory. Frank's choices are based primarily on information that he retrieves from memory. This information will be worthwhile to the extent that it can be used in evaluating available options. For instance, Frank was exposed to information from objective sources such as *Consumer Reports* magazine and this was subsequently encoded in his memory. Given the independent nature of this publication, when this information is retrieved from memory, it will carry a lot of weight in Frank's decision.

Most organizations measure customer satisfaction by how well they avoid customer dissatisfaction. A common mistake is to think that if a few customers complain, most are happy. How would you feel if you learned that 96 percent of your unhappy customers will not complain, and that all customers with gripes will tell them to 9 or 10 other people? That was the finding of a federal consumer products study. Multiply the number of complaints you get by 10, and you may have a more realistic picture of customer satisfaction. Multiply complaints by 100 and you may have an idea of how many people out there have heard bad things about your organisation.

Dr Ian Littman

You can have brilliant ideas, but if you can not get them across, your ideas will not get you anywhere.

Lee Iacocca

‹ Defining consumer behaviour
What influences consumer behaviour?
› Consumers' impact on marketing strategy

Consumer decision making

The traditional view of decision making is of the consumer as a rational decision maker. We'll explore this in more detail in Chapter 6, but in essence this view states that the consumer would seek information about potential decisions and carefully integrate this with what he or she already knows about the product. They would then weigh the pros and cons of each alternative and arrive at a decision. The five stages in this process have been described as:

- problem recognition
- information search
- judgment
- decision making
- post-decision processes.

This process of decision-making behaviour is very valid and occurs every day; however, it primarily applies when the purchase is one that is important to the consumer in some way – for example, the product is expensive, or it could impact on their health or self-image in some way. Alternatively, when consumers are making decisions about inexpensive products, such as chewing gum or soda, they do not usually follow such a complicated process. For these types of products, consumers tend to experience problem recognition and then make a decision without taking time to collect a lot of information or evaluate the alternatives. Given the low levels of financial risk, consumers usually try inexpensive products then evaluate them after **trial**.[9]

Problem recognition and information search

Consumers identify a 'problem' when their existing state differs from their ideal state. In other words, they have an existing need or desire that is unfulfilled. To return to our iPhone example, Frank knows that his existing phone lacks several features that he desires, such as an MP3 player and a personal organiser. Since his existing state is different from his ideal state, Frank recognises that he has a problem. In order to resolve this problem, Frank engages in a search for alternative products that could meet his needs. His search provides insight into the different mobile phones that possess the brand, functionality and cost **attribute**s that he wants.

This may seem simple, but you need to give customers what they want, not what you think they want. And, if you do this, people will keep coming back.

John Ilhan

Judgment and decision making

Once the problem has been identified and a search for desirable alternatives has been completed, the consumer must now evaluate the alternatives and make a decision based on the possible options. Frank's decision requires a great deal of effort since the iPhone involves both a significant financial cost and a significant time investment (because he must sign a two-year contract). Given this risk, Frank is willing to spend a lot of time and mental effort in making this decision. He identifies important criteria that he can use to evaluate his planned purchase. Then he will decide whether this brand best satisfies his needs.

Post-decision processes

Once the decision is made and the product is purchased, the last step in the decision-making process is evaluating the outcome – is the consumer satisfied with the product or service? Based on the response to this question the consumer could react in different ways. For instance, if Frank is satisfied with his iPhone purchase he could react positively and recommend it to his friends; he could also purchase another iPhone in the future when Apple release an upgraded version of the phone. If he is dissatisfied, he could react negatively and complain to Apple; he could also post public complaints online or he could return the phone. A company's response to customer complaints can have a significant impact on its success. On average, a customer who is dissatisfied shares their negative feelings with approximately ten other individuals.

Running glossary

attribute
a quality or feature regarded as a characteristic or inherent part of someone or something

trial
a test of the performance, qualities, or suitability of someone or something

Why should marketers be interested in consumer behaviour? Why should understanding the processes underlying consumer behaviour matter to businesses all over the globe? The answer to these questions is nearly always: because understanding how consumers behave leads to greater profitability.

One definition of marketing is 'satisfying consumers' needs profitably'. This can only occur if marketers understand what their consumers' needs are and how they will respond if provided with certain product offerings to satisfy these needs. How consumers respond to a firm's products and services is the true **litmus test** of a marketing strategy. Gathering information about consumers helps companies to clearly identify their target market and to assess any possible threats and potential opportunities for their product or service. This data also enables the company to build a base of core consumers who are loyal to the brand and allows them the opportunity to establish long-term relationships with their target market.

Developing information about consumer behaviour

Market research is the process by which marketing information is collected, synthesised and analysed. It is an expensive and time-consuming process that needs to be very carefully budgeted and scheduled. It should be used when there is time to properly gather, assess and act on the information. For instance, if Virgin Mobile wants to introduce a new type of smart phone but they have not yet conducted the research, they must weigh their desire to get the new product to market quickly against the need to conduct research regarding which types of features consumers would desire in such a phone. Research is a fundamental tool used by marketers to gain insight into target segments being served. There are two major types of marketing research methodologies: **qualitative** and **quantitative** research.

No great marketing decisions have ever been made on quantitative data.
John Scully

Qualitative and quantitative

Qualitative research methods are used in the early stages of assessing the marketing environment. These research methods include in-depth interviews that use **open-ended** questions to promote lots of interaction between the researcher and the respondent. Focus groups can also be used for qualitative research; these usually take the form of a loosely structured discussion among a small group of people. Both methods are usually administered by highly trained interviewer-analysts who also evaluate the findings.

Qualitative research methods provide very rich data and allow marketing researchers to understand an individual's motivations for purchasing or consuming different products. There are some drawbacks to these research methods. The findings tend to be subjective, since only a small group of consumers are interviewed. This subjectivity makes it inappropriate to use the information for predicting the behaviour of wider populations. As a result, qualitative methods tend to be used for obtaining new ideas for promotional campaigns and products and these can later be tested more thoroughly in larger studies. An example of qualitative research is a focus group to examine why consumers would drink one brand of soft drink over another.

On the other hand, companies sometimes collect data on their customers using quantitative methods. Quantitative research methods are used by researchers to understand the effects of changes in different elements of the marketing mix. This allows marketers to predict consumer behaviour.

Compared to qualitative research, more structured questions are asked, and there is less interaction between the researcher and respondent. Quantitative research methods include experiments, surveys and observation. The results are descriptive, but can be used to predict how groups of consumers might behave. In addition, if the data is collected randomly, then the results can be generalised and applied to larger populations.

Running glossary

litmus test
a decisively indicative test

open-ended
having no predetermined limit or boundary

qualitative
relating to, measuring, or measured by the quality of something rather than its quantity

quantitative
relating to, measuring, or measured by the quantity of something rather than its quality

〈 What influences consumer behaviour?
Consumers' impact on marketing strategy
〉 Methods of data collection

Primary and secondary data

In completing marketing research, marketers must address two major questions:

1
What sources of data should be used?

2
How should the data be collected?

Marketing research data can be sourced from inside and outside the firm. **Primary** data is collected by individual researchers or organisations to answer specific research questions. **Secondary** data is information that has already been collected by another person or organisation.

Primary sources are effective for collecting data on marketing variables that are under the company's control. For example, if Manchester United Football Club wants to design new shirts for their younger supporters, they would be well-advised to gather information directly from the supporters (consumers) themselves.

Running glossary

primary
not derived from, caused by, or based on anything else

secondary
coming after, less important than, or resulting from someone or something else that is primary

The Nissan Pure

Marketing research is an essential part of marketing management. Automobile manufacturers have always been at the cutting edge of research and design. Nissan North America has developed an innovative approach to integrating original research and ideas in their automobile deign. The company launched a programme called Sweat Equity Enterprises (SEE), which brought together 18 high school students to develop a concept for a low-cost vehicle, which would be targeted towards youth in metropolitan areas. The students worked with Nissan Design America designer Bryan Thompson to conduct market research, predict upcoming trends and produce detailed professional-quality designs for the car's exterior, accessories and interior elements. The students came up with six car concepts, which were then submitted to Nissan. Nissan chose the Pure concept vehicle designed by Chris Jones, Paul Ayala, Alex Rodriguez and Shakirra Torain. The designs were so well received that Nissan created digital animated models of all six designs, and a three-foot professional model of Pure, which they revealed at the Los Angeles Auto Show in November 2007.[10]

Secondary data sources are not always the best source of information about specific customer needs but can provide useful insights at times. For instance, before the London Eye was opened, the London Tourism Authority (LTA) wanted to determine the best times for operation. Secondary data revealed the months when most tourists visited London, and meteorological data provided weather predictions that would aid the LTA in determining the best months to operate the Eye, enabling them to make an informed decision without conducting their own primary research.

Secondary data can be both internal, such as financial statements and customer letters to the company, or external, such as census data and online search engine results. In spite of the fact that secondary data might not fit the categories or definitions that marketers need for the specific research question, it is much less expensive to obtain than primary data and it can be obtained very quickly.

For both primary and secondary types of data sources, the information that is collected must be of high quality. Both types of sources (and especially secondary data), must possess the following qualities:

- Relevance
- Accuracy
- Currency
- Impartiality

Gerber uses qualitative research

The Gerber Products Company uses observational research to determine babies' reactions to their baby food. They test new ingredients and flavours in the Gerber Lab and use their observations to modify existing products or create new products. For example, this research led to the company removing oregano from the firm's Italian Spaghetti baby food.[11]

Authentic marketing is not the art of selling what you make but knowing what to make. It is the art of identifying and understanding customer needs and creating solutions that deliver satisfaction to the customers, profits to the producers and benefits for the stakeholders.

Philip Kotler

Marketers use a number of different primary research tools to collect information from consumers. Some are based on what consumers say and others are based on what they do. These tools all provide different types of data and there are different benefits to using each method.

Online data collection

The Internet enables companies to overcome two disadvantages of survey research: cost and speed. Internet surveys can collect data quickly and at minimal cost to the company. Internet websites such as Survey Monkey <www.surveymonkey.com> have been established to aid companies in collecting survey data. This company claims to collect data 75% faster than traditional survey methods.

Surveys

One research tool with which we are probably all familiar is the survey. This is an instrument that asks consumers to respond to a predetermined set of questions. Some survey questions may be open-ended and may help identify possible motivations to consumer actions. These questions may ask consumers to fill in the blanks, for example, 'tell us about your last experience travelling on a British Airways flight'. Others might be closed-ended and ask consumers to use a rating scale, for example, 'on a scale of 1–10, how much do you like to fly British Airways?'. Surveys can be conducted in person, by mail, over the phone or on the Internet.

Key issues to be addressed when completing survey research include: questionnaire design (for example, how many questions will be on the survey? What will the phrasing be?); sampling (who are the respondents? How will they be chosen?) and data analysis (how will you tabulate, summarise and draw inferences from the data?).

Asked about the power of advertising in research surveys, most agree that it works, but not on them.
Eric Clark

Focus groups

Focus groups see a marketing researcher meet with groups of consumers in either a formal or informal setting. Consumers are encouraged to share their feelings about their needs or reactions to different products and services. The researcher serves only as a moderator of the discussion.

However, unlike surveys (which can be used to collect input from a large number of people) focus groups bring together much smaller groups of 6–12 consumers to discuss an issue or offering. Focus groups provide in-depth qualitative insights into consumer attitudes, compared to the largely numerical (quantitative) results provided by survey methods. Most focus groups are conducted in person; however, researchers have discovered that the anonymity provided by telephone or computer-based focus groups allow respondents to be more open about their feelings. These methods are especially useful for topics that could be considered personal or embarrassing.

Interviews

Similar to focus groups, interviews involve direct contact with consumers. Interviews tend to be better suited to topics that are sensitive, confidential or emotionally charged. They tend to be used when researchers want to collect more detailed information and to truly understand consumers' motivations. Interviews usually require a trained interviewer who tries to establish a **rapport** with consumers. Interviews provide a great deal of information but they are one of the more time-consuming and costly methods of conducting research.

Running glossary

rapport
a close and harmonious relationship in which the people or groups concerned understand each other's feelings or ideas and communicate well

< Consumers' impact on marketing strategy
Methods of data collection
> Case study: The case of Coke Zero

Experiments

In experimental procedures the researcher manipulates one or more **variable**s (for example, different price levels for weekend flights to European cities from London) to allow measurement of its effect on other variables of interest (such as the consumer demand for these weekend flights). By controlling other elements of the environment (in this case, the hypothetical competitors' prices) the researcher would be able to establish whether low prices caused a subsequent increase or decrease in demand for the weekend flights of their company.

Non-experimental procedures do not involve the manipulation of any variables by the researcher. For example, if a consumer is asked, 'What would you like about travelling by plane to Rome for a weekend getaway?', then it is not experimental because the researcher has not changed any variables that could impact the consumer's response. Issues to be considered when conducting experimental research include: which factor will be the variable that will be manipulated; which extraneous variables need to be considered (the external factors that need to be controlled to avoid affecting the results); and should the experiments be conducted in lab or in the field?

Computer-generated virtual shopping environments

One global software company, GMI, boasts that they provide 'integrated solutions for marketing intelligence'. GMI developed a virtual shopping environment in which customers 'walk down the aisles', 'pick up products' and 'add products to shopping baskets' if they choose to. This virtual environment allows the company's clients the opportunity to experiment with various packages, prices or layouts to determine which would be most effective in motivating customer purchase.[12]

Any communication or marketing professional needs cross-cultural research and communication skills to be able to succeed in the future.
Marye Tharp

What do marketers learn from consumer research?

Consumer research not only helps marketers identify and define marketing problems but it also helps to define opportunities too. In addition, research results help marketers generate and evaluate potential solutions in the form of marketing actions. These marketing actions might include how the firm should **segment** its market, as well as how it can make decisions about the **marketing mix**.

How should the market be segmented and targeted?

Marketing research enables marketers to determine which groups of customers exist in the market. Research helps companies generate profiles of these customers and allows them to place these customers in groups of similar individuals who will respond in a similar fashion to marketing stimuli. Research also allows marketers to know the size and potential profitability of each segment.

Understanding consumer behaviour allows marketers to determine which segments would be best for them to target with their products and services. By conducting research, companies can discover which segments have needs that could be best satisfied by the company.

Marketing research also aids in making strategic decisions such as product-positioning (how the products should be perceived by the consumer). Consumer research can help managers understand how consumers perceive and categorise different brands in the marketplace. This allows them to see how consumers view other brands in relation to their own brand and to determine whether or not their brand should be repositioned.

Running glossary

marketing mix
probably the most famous marketing term. Its elements are the basic, tactical components of a marketing plan. Also known as the Four P's, the marketing mix elements are price, place, product, and promotion

market segment
subgroup of people or organisations sharing one or more characteristics that cause them to have similar product needs

variable
a factor that can be changed or adapted

〈 Consumers' impact on marketing strategy
Methods of data collection
〉 Case study: The case of Coke Zero

Changing the marketing mix

In addition to the product itself, consumer research allows the company to address issues related to the marketing mix.
For example, what should the advertising look like? Which visuals should be used? What should the message be? When should the advertising run?

Research also allows marketers to understand how consumers respond to price changes and to use this information in their pricing decisions. Finally it allows marketers the opportunity to determine how best the offering should be distributed.
How do we get the offering to the consumer?

Ethical issues in consumer research

Marketers rely heavily on consumer research to create and sell goods and services that satisfy consumers' needs.

This research allows organisations to generate better-designed products, better customer service and react to any failed products. An additional benefit of consumer research is that it is helpful in identifying ways in which companies can establish and enhance their relationships with their customers.

On the other hand, research costs money and in several cases leads to an increase in the cost of producing the product and a higher price for the customer. A more serious concern involves the invasion of consumers' privacy. Companies who want to be close to their customers often collect data about them. This leads to a fear that marketers may have too much information about their customer's consumption practices. The United States Government has recently taken steps to prevent companies from tracking consumers on the Internet. Individuals can now opt out from all such websites.

I notice increasing reluctance on the part of marketing executives to use judgment; they are coming to rely too much on research, and they use it as a drunkard uses a lamp post. For support, rather than for illumination.

David Ogilvy

Augusta National Golf Club

Some researchers introduce bias into their research. This tends to happen when studies are commissioned by companies or organisations seeking to justify a particular position. For example, between 2002 and 2005 the Augusta National Golf Club was under pressure because of a perceived gender bias in their membership policies. The club hosts the annual Masters Golf Tournament in the US, but only admitted its first black member in 1990 and, as of 2009 had not accepted a female member (although women are able to play the course as guests). The club was faced with high-profile protests in 2002 when the chairperson of the National Council of Women's Organizations, Martha Burk, publicly challenged the club's membership policy. Up to that time, IBM, Coca-Cola and Citigroup sponsored the tournament but they all pulled their commercial support for the 2003 Masters tournament and the tournament remained without a corporate sponsor until 2005.

Faced with losing major sponsorship deals, the club conducted a national study and the results appeared to confirm that members of the general public preferred for women not to be granted membership of the club.

However, on closer inspection, it is clear that the club's research had been conducted with a bias to suit the club's own views.

The first questions within the research dealt with the constitution of the United States. Respondents were asked whether they believed in the sanctity of the American constitution, and further questions addressed the golf club's constitutional right as a private club to choose its own members. By asking leading questions in such a way, the club was able to come to a conclusion that suited its beliefs.[13]

< Methods of data collection
Case study / **The case of Coke Zero**
> Questions and exercises

Background

In June 2005, the Coca-Cola Company launched a new brand called Coke Zero. The drink was sweetened partly with a blend of aspartame and acesulfame potassium. Aspartame is a key ingredient in Diet Coke, but because of the added sweetener, Coke Zero was marketed as tasting more like original Coke than its diet derivative.[14]

Even with the multiple varieties of Coke on the market, officials at Coca-Cola were not worried about market confusion. They believed that consumers were becoming more interested in variety and that the multiple variations of Coke could coexist.

The company launched Coke Zero using a unique marketing campaign. Coke Zero was targeted primarily to young adult males. This resulted in different positioning in North America compared to Europe. Globally, Coke Zero was marketed as a 'diet' drink with zero sugar. However, in the United States and Canada, it was marketed as having 'zero calories' since to younger men in North America, diet drinks are viewed as being meant only for older, female consumers.[15]

Marketing Coke Zero in the United States

In the United States, the marketing focus was on the similarity between the taste of Coke Zero and 'classic' Coke. The advertising campaign was based on the premise that executives at Coca-Cola selling the Coke Classic brand planned to sue their colleagues selling Coke Zero. The advertisements used real lawyers who were unaware that they were being recorded. The executives in charge of the flagship brand pretended that they wanted to initiate a lawsuit against Coke Zero for 'taste infringement'. They claimed that Coke Zero 'taste(d) too much like the Classic Coke soft drink'. The advertising campaign proved to be a success. One commercial shows a lawyer (unaware of the joke) telling two actors portraying Coke Classic executives: 'It'll be dismissed. You'll be humiliated'.

This ad campaign included video clips posted on social networking websites such as Twitter and YouTube, as well as ads posted on website banners. In addition to helping to position the new brand as contemporary and 'young', the Punk'd-style advertising strategy effectively reached the young male target group.

**Coke offers a wide variety
of choice within a single brand**
Coke works hard at minimising
confusion by making sure all of
their brands have distinct graphics
and marketing.

< Methods of data collection
Case study / The case of Coke Zero
> Questions and exercises

Marketing Coke Zero around the world

The success of the marketing campaign in the United States led to Coca-Cola using similar strategies around the world. One cornerstone of the campaign was the creation of a group called The Zero Movement. This group was promoted on a blog on which a young man rants about why life is so full of stuff to do and how it would be so much nicer if there was, well, 'zero to do'. The blog concluded with several supportive comments, which made it appear to be an individual's site rather than a promotional tool.

In Australia the campaign generated a lot of interest in Coke Zero until consumer advocates discovered that The Zero Movement was part of the Coca-Cola marketing campaign. A counter blog, The Zero Coke Movement, was established to expose the perceived lack of ethics in this advertising strategy. In addition, other blogs such as The Zero Movement Sucks were started. After this controversy, logos and other Coke Zero branding were uploaded on the website. This made it very clear that the website was linked to Coca-Cola. In spite of this controversy (or perhaps because of it) Coke Zero's Australian launch proved a resounding success.

Question 1

The Coca-Cola Company utilised different strategies in Europe and Australia compared to North America. In Europe Coke Zero was positioned as a 'diet drink' and in North America it was positioned as a 'low-calorie drink'. Do you believe this was an appropriate strategy? Could Coke have used the same positioning strategy in both geographic areas? If so, which should they have used? If not, why?

Question 2

This case discusses some aspects of the study of consumer behaviour that have drawn criticism from some observers. Coke Zero created a 'fake blog' to generate interest in The Zero Movement. Was this unethical?

Question 3

Coke used celebrity endorsers for Coke Zero in Europe, including Cheryl Cole and Wayne Rooney. In addition, the company initiated a marketing tie-in with a James Bond movie released in 2008, *Quantum of Solace*. Are these promotion strategies appropriate for Coke Zero? Do the spokespersons match the image that Coke Zero is trying to promote?

Coke Zero

Coke Zero was launched by the Coca-Cola Company in October 2006. This product was Coca-Cola's biggest launch in 22 years and was targeted primarily to young males.

Discussion questions

1

Describe the different factors
that impact consumer behaviour.
Which of these factors do you believe
would have the greatest impact on
how consumers behave?

2

Why should marketers be interested
in consumer behaviour?

3

What is motivation and how could
it impact consumer behaviour?

4

What are the major differences
between qualitative and
quantitative data?

5

What are the different methods
of collecting data when conducting
marketing research? What are the
advantages of each method?

6

In addition to the issues cited in the
text, what other ethical issues could
be raised by how consumer research
is conducted?

Exercise 1

Ask a friend to identify his or her
favourite possession and conduct
an in-depth interview with them to
determine the underlying reasons for
his or her choice. Why is this object
so important? Is any other object
as important to them?

Next, create a survey that could
elicit the same information from
another friend. Collect the data from
your second friend using the survey.
Do the results differ? Are there
any advantages to collecting the
information using one research
method versus the other?

Endnotes

1
'iPhone calls to some business users', The Wall Street Journal, 24 July 2007

2
'iPhone owners crying foul over price cut', The New York Times, 7 September 2007

3
Hoyer, W. and MacInnis D. (2007) *Consumer Behavior*, (4 ed) Boston: Houghton Mifflin

4
Adapted from conceptual model of consumer behaviour, Hoyer, W. and MacInnis D. (2007) *Consumer Behavior*, (4 ed) Boston: Houghton Mifflin

5
Global Industry Analysts. *Consumer Electronics Market Research Report 2008*

6
<www.nielsenmedia.com>

7
Mitchell T. R. (1982) 'Motivation: New Directions for Theory, Research and Practice'; *The Academy of Management Review*, Vol. 7, No. 1. (1982), pp. 80–88

8
Bearden W. O. and Teel J. E. (1983) 'Selected Determinants of Consumer Satisfaction and Complaint Reports'; *Journal of Marketing Research*, Vol. 20, No. 1

9
Krugman, H. E. 'The Impact of Television Advertising: Learning without Involvement'; *Public Opinion Quarterly*, Fall 1965

10
Patton, P. 'Cars with Street Cred (Students Dreamed Them Up.)'; *The New York Times*, 7 October 2007

11
Brooks, G. 'It's Goo, Goo, Goo, Goo Vibrations at the Gerber Baby Lab'; *The Wall Street Journal*, 4 December 1996

12
<www.gmi-mr.com>

13
Pennington, B. 'At Augusta National, the Lines have been drawn'; *The New York Times*, 10 April 2003

14
'Coke to launch new no-calorie soda'; *Associated Press*, 21 March 2005

15
Elliott S. 'Can't Tell Your Cokes Apart? Sue Someone'; *The New York Times*, 5 March 2007

Exercise 2

Imagine you are a marketing manager for Starbucks. You need consumer research to support future decisions about additional menu items and promotions. Which research methods would you use to uncover the answers to the following questions and why?

Consider the following:

■ Do customers prefer Starbucks coffee over those of its main competitors?
■ Would Starbucks sell more coffee if the company lowered its prices?
■ Would using coupons positively impact sales?

Low-context culture

Many overt and explicit messages that are simple and clear.

Outer locus of control and blame of others for failure.

More focus on verbal communication than body language.

Visible, external, outward reaction.

Flexible and open grouping patterns, changing as needed.

Fragile bonds between people with little sense of loyalty.

Low commitment to relationship. Task more important than relationships.

Time is highly organised. Product is more important than process.

Characteristics of high and low cultural context

High- and low-context cultures vary on several dimensions, including use of non-verbal signals, the directness of communication and the perception of time and space. All of these variables could impact marketing strategies targeting groups from different cultural contexts.[2]

Targeting immigrant groups is impacted by level of acculturation

Related to the concept of high or low context is the idea of **acculturation**. Many immigrants in the United States, and in some European countries, come from high-context cultures, whereas the majority population tend to be low context. When developing marketing strategies, businesses need to be aware of how much of the original culture these immigrants have maintained. Some immigrants **assimilate** into the majority culture and quickly adopt their norms, and behaviours (including consumer behaviours).

Others undergo a process of partial acculturation. This is the adaptation to one country's culture by someone from another country.[3] Many immigrants hold on to the beliefs and practices from their original culture and do not fully adopt the practices of their new home. This can prove difficult for marketers who are targeting these groups, since they may not be fully aware of the cultural differences between the groups and may not be able to create effective marketing strategies as a result.

Targeted product design

In the US, Interstate Bakeries Corporation is a well-known manufacturer of snack foods, including Twinkies, CupCakes and Ding Dongs. In order to target the growing Hispanic market, the company launched a new line of snacks specifically designed with the Hispanic consumer in mind. The line was launched under the Hostess brand, and appropriately named *Las Delicias de Hostess*. The new line included ten new snack cakes. It featured *pastelitos* (cakes flavoured with pineapple, strawberry or chocolate); *panque* (mini-pound cakes with strawberry and pineapple fillings); cupcakes with pineapple or *dulce de leche* fillings; and *concha* (a chewy yeast roll with sugar topping). These snacks all contain fillings or flavours that are traditionally popular with Hispanics.[4]

accommodation theory
efforts on the part of the communicator to make themselves as similar as possible to their audience in order to improve communication

acculturation
the adaptation to one country's culture by someone from another country

assimilate
absorb and integrate (people, ideas, or culture) into a wider society or culture

Targeted advertising and promotion

Advertising and promotion strategies are also influenced by the preferences of the target group. This becomes much more salient in the case of ethnic groups whose cultural norms and tastes are different from the majority group in the society. Promotion strategies designed for wider society may not be effective in targeting specific ethnic or social groups. The cultural norms of the target market must be taken into consideration when designing promotion strategies.

For instance, in many Asian cultures white is the traditional colour of sorrow and mourning. So, when creating a commercial for life insurance services targeted at older Asian consumers in the UK, images of models wearing black at a funeral may not be appropriate. Additionally, **accommodation theory** would dictate that the spokespersons in commercials directed to specific ethnic groups should look like the target audience. This can result in a more favourable response from the audience.

America's population will increase by 50% over the next fifty years, with almost 90% of that increase in the minority community. Both Fortune 1000 and minority businesses need to pay attention to the consumer purchasing power that will result from that growth.

Norman Y. Mineta

Accommodation theory

This theory states that attempts made by a communicator to make themselves more like the people they are addressing are noticed and appreciated by the audience. So, as the sender increases similarity to the receiver, the probability that the receiver will like the sender increases.

In the area of consumer behaviour, this would mean that the greater the 'accommodation' by advertisers, the more favourable the consumer's response would be to these targeted messages. Accommodation could mean the use of language or symbols with which the targeted group is familiar or use of models or spokespersons that look like the members of the targeted group.

The level of acculturation of the target group impacts the effects of accommodation. Generally, the less acculturated the ethnic group, the more likely they would be to respond positively to targeted advertising. Groups that do not identify strongly with their ethnic identity would not react as favourably to accommodation efforts, for example, if the advertiser uses models that look like them.

A word of warning

If they get it wrong, however, companies risk being perceived as patronising, or even racist, in their attempts to include different ethnic groups in their advertising. This was the case with Cadbury Schweppes' 2007 Trident chewing gum adverts. The company released five adverts that included a black man speaking with a heavy, almost caricature, Caribbean accent. The campaign was called 'mastication for the nation' and Cadbury claimed it was meant to celebrate the dub poets in the UK and highlight the multicultural nature of British society. The campaign received 519 complaints shortly after being launched. Research showed that one in five British African-Caribbean persons interviewed found the ads offensive. The Advertising Standards Authority ruled that Cadbury Schweppes had breached rules on offensive and harmful stereotypes. In the end, Cadbury Schweppes apologised for the campaign and pulled the ads. These missteps highlight the need for firms to conduct adequate research and to be responsive to research results when targeting different ethnic groups.[5]

L'Oreal and the African-American female consumer

Over the past decade, one of the world's largest cosmetics companies, L'Oreal, has transformed itself from a French company focused on just one target market into a global business with skin, hair and cosmetic products tailored to consumers from Dallas to Delhi. L'Oreal has developed the knack for buying local cosmetics brands and changing them so that they have a more global appeal. While doing so, L'Oreal still maintains the product's appeal to the specific local tastes. In spite of its origins, L'Oreal is French only when it wants to be. The rest of the time it's satisfied with being African, Asian, or anything else that sells.[6] In the late 1990s, L'Oreal turned its attention to the growing ethnic-beauty market in the United States. In 2008, this market had an estimated annual value of $14.7 billion. Most companies that have dominated ethnic beauty care in the US have maintained close contact with their customers and are in tune with their desires and the trends in this market.

L'Oreal bought two such companies, SoftSheen and Carson, and integrated them into a single entity that the company sees as being very competitive for the African-American consumer. 'You can't pretend to be No. 1 in the world,' says Alain Evrard, L'Oreal's managing director for Africa, 'and forget about 1 billion consumers of African origin.'[7]

In order to promote their new line, L'Oreal hired famous African-American celebrities, such as Beyonce Knowles, as spokespersons. The singer signed a $4.7 million endorsement deal in 2004 to promote the new line of products. L'Oreal recognised the importance of targeting different ethnic groups and is now reaping the financial rewards.

Religious subcultures

Religion can also have a major impact on consumer behaviour. Religion impacts on the values and behaviour of many individuals. It establishes a set of beliefs and dictates norms of behaviour. In some societies these are so binding that deviating from these norms is punishable by law. In other smaller religious subcultures, such as Catholics in the United States, behaviour that is considered out of the norm can result in social censure. Religion can impact on an individual consumer's decision making on anything from the food they eat, to the clothes they wear.

Given the number of consumers for whom religion is important, some marketers have chosen to specifically target these groups with their marketing efforts. Two key areas where religion could impact marketing activities are promotion and the product itself.

The 'Fulla' doll

In the Middle East many parents are concerned by an over-abundance of western toys. Dolls are of particular concern, especially Barbie, who is often seen dressed in little more than a bikini. Given the strict standards of dress followed by many Muslims in the Middle East, toys of this nature are simply inappropriate. In response, a company in Egypt manufactured an alternative that would be acceptable to Muslims. The doll, named 'Fulla', is dressed in an Islamic headscarf and Muslim overcoat and carries a pink felt prayer rug. Launched in 2003, the doll quickly became a hit in Egypt and then grew in popularity in other Middle Eastern countries.[8]

How can marketers target religious subcultures?

Companies targeting groups of religious consumers can use several types of media promotions to reach these individuals. For example, there are numerous Christian television stations on which marketers can buy advertising space. Premier Media, a large Christian media group in the UK, sells advertising on their radio and television stations, and also on their websites and magazines. These ads reach millions of Christians who view the different media offered by this group on a daily basis. Premier Media promises to deliver a substantial and growing audience that is 'uniquely loyal, involved and responsive' and which trusts the messages they receive from Premier Media. One such listener stated: 'I am a regular listener to Premier Radio and have found great comfort, information and encouragement through the station over the years. I must emphasise that as a Christian, there aren't many resources available to encourage my faith and entertain me in a positive way.'[9] This kind of very loyal, engaged listener is likely to be open to advertising 'approved' by the radio station.

In addition to targeted promotions, companies can also manufacture products specifically for particular religious groups. There are many stores that sell halal foods targeted to Muslims and kosher foods targeted to Jewish consumers. These foods are prepared using very strict religious practices. Additionally, products are manufactured for sale on special religious holidays like Eid ul-Fitr celebrated by Muslims, Divali celebrated by Hindus and Christmas and Easter for Christians.

Marketers must also be aware that some images are considered offensive by some religions. There have been several well-publicised incidents in recent years of companies that manufactured products containing elements which some religions found offensive. For example, in the 1990s Jewish groups protested the work of designer Jean-Paul Gaultier. He raised their ire when he used traditional Hasidic men's costumes as inspiration for women's clothes.[10]

Marketers must not only be sensitive to the needs of their target market, but also the general public at large. The question must be asked, 'Would large segments of society be offended by the products that we sell or the way that we sell them?' If the answer is 'yes', companies must seriously consider scrapping such ideas.

A group can be defined as 'two or more individuals who share a common purpose'. Group members tend to share the same values, recognise that the group members have to work together in some way, assume specific roles, and can provide reward or punishment.

For marketers, reference groups are very important. A reference group is a group that serves as a point of comparison (or reference) for an individual. The group's beliefs and behaviours establish norms of behaviour for the individual and can affect everything from the food they purchase to the activities that they enjoy.

Associative reference groups

These are groups to which we belong. **Associative reference groups** can require either formal membership, as in a university class, or informal membership, as in a group of friends who meet regularly at a local pub. One group requires certain formal activities before membership is allowed. In the case of the class, you would first need to matriculate at the university, and then sign up for the class. Any prerequisites, must also be completed. For informal groups, there is no official path to entry. You could become a member of the above-mentioned informal group simply by showing up at irregular intervals at your local pub. Marketers can use both types of group to exert influence on individuals to make purchases. For example, marketers who target college students often rely on the influence of peer groups to impact the choices of these individuals who want to dress and look like each other.

Running glossary

aspirational reference groups
groups to which we would like to belong, but currently are not members

associative reference groups
formal or informal groups to which we belong

dissociative reference groups
groups to which we do not want to belong that have values and attitudes that we do not wish to emulate

No matter what your product is, you are ultimately in the education business. Your customers need to be constantly educated about the many advantages of doing business with you, trained to use your products more effectively, and taught how to make never-ending improvement in their lives.
Robert G. Allen

Aspirational reference groups

These are groups to which we would like to belong, but currently are not members. These are usually groups we hold in high esteem; we sometimes pattern our behaviour after them since we want to be like them. This can be particularly true for the youth market who might want to dress and behave like their favourite music or film star. Marketers try to associate products with **aspirational reference groups**. If they are aware of the groups to which consumers aspire to belong, they may use members of that group in their advertising. In this way, consumers may associate membership of that aspirational group with the product itself.

For example, many children in England admire the English national football team and have childhood dreams of playing for the team at some point. The English Football Association has used this to their advantage. One of their biggest sellers is their football shirt for children. These young consumers are driven to look like their idols on the national team, especially during international competitions like the World Cup.

Dissociative reference groups

These are groups to which we do not want to belong because they have values and attitudes that we do not wish to emulate. For example, many people in the United States look down upon fans of NASCAR racing, who are typically younger males from the south-eastern United States. They are perceived by some to be uncultivated and somewhat boorish. Even though NASCAR racing is increasing in popularity, the promoters of NASCAR have an uphill battle given that their primary consumers are a **dissociative reference group**.

NASCAR promoters have therefore initiated efforts to increase and diversify their target market. One such strategy is the NASCAR reality show, *NASCAR Drivers: 360*. Since its launch in May 2004, NASCAR has seen an increase in the number of female fans to events. They have also experienced a greater number of fans who come from further north in the United States.[11]

Unwanted associations

Several football teams in Spain and Italy have had trouble attracting sponsorship because of the increase in neo-Nazi and fascist salutes during their football games. If a product is linked to a dissociative group, it becomes very difficult for marketers to successfully promote the product.

How reference groups influence behaviour

The beliefs and consumption practices of a reference group can influence a consumer's behaviour. Individuals take cues from reference groups when they are purchasing anything from clothing to automobiles. Usually, reference groups influence consumers in two main ways: **normative influence** and **informational influence**.

Using experts to create informational influence

Marketers use experts in the field related to their product in order to exert informational influence. If a source is regarded as an expert in a given product category, this increases the credibility of that source to the consumer. Adidas and other athletic shoe companies use famous sportsmen as spokespersons for their products. Tracy McGrady, one of the top young players in the NBA, endorsed a basketball shoe for Adidas. This added instant credibility to the new shoe; as a successful basketball player he must know a lot about this type of footwear.

Normative influence

This occurs when a consumer performs an action in order to conform to another person's expectations. This influence is driven by established norms of behaviour – what is acceptable to society. The reference group that exerts normative influence derives this power through its ability to reward or punish the individual's behaviour. Normative influence can affect the products we choose to purchase, for example we may buy certain types of clothing so as to avoid ridicule (or receive compliments) from our friends.

Products that are consumed in public tend to be more susceptible to normative influence. If a product is consumed privately there is no reward or punishment from the group. Goods and services that are consumed publicly are likely to lead to more immediate and spontaneous reward or punishment. For example, normative influence is less likely for products such as mattresses or antiperspirants that are consumed in private. But products that are consumed publicly provide the opportunity for the consumption experience to be observed. These include clothing, automobiles and jewellery.

For marketers, this means showing the rewards for using their product and what the 'punishment' would be for non-use. Some ads for personal hygiene products indicate that others would evaluate us in a favourable manner socially if we use the product.

Informational influence

This occurs when someone else provides information to the consumer to help them make a purchase decision. This information is often based on personal experience; friends recommending tried and tested products that they believe will perform well. This can save the consumer considerable time and money both before and after a purchase – before, since it cuts down on required search time; after, since a reliable product would incur fewer repair and replacement costs.

To put this into context, if you were looking for a new laptop you might seek advice from a knowledgable friend. Given the financial risk involved, their recommendation would go a long way to convincing you about which brand and model to purchase.

Informational influence tends to have significant impact given the high value consumers place on word of mouth communication, especially when the source is someone we know personally. We trust that our friends and relatives will not mislead us.

Products that are complex tend to lend themselves to informational influence. A considerable amount of learning may be required before these products are purchased. Instead of investing that time towards in-depth research, consumers often choose to use the advice of others who are already experts in that area. Consumers also tend to approach others for information when there is some risk involved in the purchase – whether that risk is to their finances, health or social life. The following products would lend themselves to informational influence: houses (financial); paediatric care (health); hair stylist (social).

Marketers therefore seek to create a situation whereby they control the flow of information to the consumer. For example, the producer of the hit independent movie *Cowboy Bebop* hired young movie viewers to create blogs and visit chat boards online to recommend the movie to others seeking information.[12] This creates an ethical dilemma since consumers online may believe that these are independent reviews; this adds to the source's credibility. However, the source in this case is actually employed by the company. Is this ethical? What do you think?

Running glossary

informational influence
when someone else provides information to the consumer that the consumer then considers when making a purchase decision

normative influence
when a consumer performs an action in order to conform to another person's expectations

〈 Reference groups
Consumer-related reference groups
〉Case study: McDonald's goes global

There are many different kinds of reference groups, and there are some that exist specifically for consumers. These groups can revolve around shopping; others are created because the members all admire a certain brand, such as Harley-Davidson, for example; and yet still others are based around a certain activity, for example video-game playing and movie viewing. Since these groups tend to be very familiar with the product category or brand, they can be vital to companies when conducting marketing research. They are often able to provide constructive feedback to companies regarding their products and services. Additionally, some of these groups are very brand-loyal, so they can also be a great place to market **brand extension**s. Such a captive market can be important when a company is trying to launch a new product or an extension of an existing product.

Shopping groups

These can be either informal or formal groups. Groups of female friends may get together for shopping trips to buy shoes or clothing. These tend to be social events where emphasis is placed on spending time together as well as finding good bargains. Group members usually look to each other for recommendations regarding potential purchases. A more formal group is a shopping cooperative. In this type of group, members may pool their resources together in order to buy in bulk from wholesalers at reduced prices. These types of cooperatives were first popular with small farmers and businesses in the United States, but became more popular with private consumers once they recognised the financial benefit of buying items in bulk. It is now possible to join large wholesale cooperatives and simply pay a membership fee to get the benefit of the wholesale price without having to join an actual group.

Running glossary

brand extension
adding a new product or service to an existing brand range in order to appeal to a different market segment

Virtual groups

These are groups that make use of the Internet in order to connect with other individuals who share similar interests. It is no longer necessary to have face-to-face interaction in order to interact with someone who shares your interests. Thus, these groups have no real geographical boundaries and can be international in scope. An example of a virtual group would be message boards where individuals can share their opinions regarding products and services. One such group would be the Yahoo Movies community. Consumers can join this website and provide anonymous reviews of current movies. Since the comments are made anonymously, group members tend to be brutally honest with their reviews.

Brand communities

One type of virtual group is a brand community. Several companies are now actively involved in establishing groups of consumers who are loyal to their brand. This leads to a long-term relationship with the consumer. These groups are very beneficial to businesses since they continue to purchase the brand and they also recommend the brand to others outside of the group. For example, Volvo established a 'Volvo saved my life' virtual community. Consumers could go online and relate their stories regarding how their Volvo cars prevented serious injury or death in an accident. This also helped to position Volvo as a safe car manufacturer. Audi also helps promote Audi drivers' clubs. These clubs are given discounts for car parts and other Audi-related products. They are also encouraged to take plant tours of Audi manufacturing operations. These activities on the companies' part help to establish an ever stronger bond between consumer and brand.

Background

McDonald's is the world's largest chain of fast food restaurants, serving approximately 50 million customers daily worldwide. The restaurants are operated by franchisees that pay rent and franchise fees to the corporation. The business was founded by brothers Dick and Mac McDonald in California, USA and was later purchased by Ray Kroc in the late 1950s. Kroc then embarked on an impressive expansion of the franchise, opening several restaurants in different states. The company became successful after focusing on providing quick meals at a moderate price to the consumer. The company continued expansion nationally in the United States and also globally. McDonald's now operates 31,000 restaurants in over 110 countries. The move into international markets has come at a price for McDonald's; the company is now known as a symbol of globalisation, and in some instances generates sentiments of anti-Americanism.[13]

McDonald's global expansion

McDonald's now has restaurants in almost every continent. In Europe alone, the company has over 6,400 restaurants. The business is growing faster in Europe than in the US and Europe is the region that provides McDonald's with the most revenue. In 2007, the company generated revenues of almost $9 billion in Europe and $8 billion in the US. This is surprising given that there are four times more outlets in the United States than in Europe. However, Europe is experiencing phenomenal growth, especially in Eastern Europe; for example in Russia they serve approximately 200,000 customers every day.

Fries with that?

McDonald's have become one of the world's biggest brands by focusing on supplying their customers with reasonably priced meals on-the-go.

The impact of culture on McDonald's operations

In Europe, under the guidance of the President of McDonald's European operations, Denis Hennequin, McDonald's has begun to focus on the customer experience more than the convenience provided by the restaurant. In the United States the restaurant's success was tied to its ability to provide a quick meal at a reasonable price. In the 'on-the-go' culture of the US, convenience and speed are valued. However, in many European countries, Denis Hennequin believed that success would be tied to 'upgrading the customer experience'.

To Hennequin, the brand positioning had to be different in different parts of the world. Acknowledging the impact of cultural differences, he believed that in the US customers tend to eat on-the-go, whereas in many parts of Europe, customers prefer to linger. For Europeans, it was about both being 'convenient and a destination place at the same time'. In order to make the McDonald's restaurants more customer-friendly, a place where someone would want to spend more time, the company underwent a major overhaul. In the 40 European countries where McDonald's does business, the company has begun to make alterations and plans to spend more than €600 million on renovations.

In many outlets, the company has replaced the red and yellow plastic signage with muted images painted in dark olive and yellow. The plastic fittings are gone, replaced with lime green designer chairs and dark leather upholstery and they are even introducing wireless Internet connectivity.

The impact of local culture is unmistakable in McDonald's European operations. In addition to a distinctly different ambience, the meals on offer also vary according to location. For example, in Rome you can order freshly cooked pasta, in France, several different French cheeses, such as Reblochon, are sometimes available. In addition, impacted by the coffee bistro culture in Europe, McDonald's is opening many McCafe's – coffee bars within another store. These shops sell gourmet coffees as well as pastries that appeal to local tastes such as flan in Spain or tortes in Germany and Austria.[14]

Fun, fast and convenient
In contrast to the European taste for long, drawn-out meals in a comfortable environment – the US McDonald's restaurants focus on offering a fun, fast and convenient meal experience.

The impact of religion on McDonald's operations

In addition to cultural norms, another major factor that impacts on the company's marketing strategy is the religion of the customer base. For example, all McDonald's restaurants in Israel serve kosher food. However, although there are over 100 McDonald's restaurants in Israel only a dozen or so are strictly kosher since they do not serve dairy and are closed on the Sabbath. In addition, McDonald's has restaurants that serve halal food. Like kosher-prepared meals, halal meals must be prepared in accordance with the relevant religious principles. In April 2007, McDonald's opened its first restaurant in London that served halal food. These attempts to satisfy religious norms have met with success; the halal restaurant in London has had visitors from all over Europe.[15]

Question 1

Does McDonald's have an appropriate global marketing strategy? What, if anything, should they change?

Question 2

Do you believe that McDonald's responds to religious influences appropriately?

Question 3

In what other ways, in addition to restaurant design and the food, could McDonald's respond to the different cultural/religious influences of the countries in which it operates?

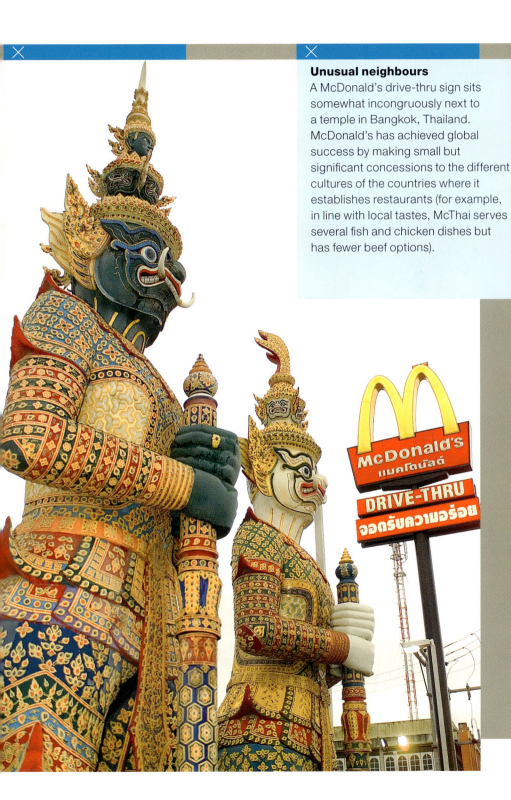

Unusual neighbours
A McDonald's drive-thru sign sits somewhat incongruously next to a temple in Bangkok, Thailand. McDonald's has achieved global success by making small but significant concessions to the different cultures of the countries where it establishes restaurants (for example, in line with local tastes, McThai serves several fish and chicken dishes but has fewer beef options).

Questions and exercises

Discussion questions

1

How would you advertise differently to consumers from a high-context culture versus a low-context culture?

2

Some immigrants do not fully assimilate into the culture of their adopted country. These groups prove difficult for marketers to target. Could you list examples of companies that have been successful in targeting immigrant populations in their new home country? What marketing strategies have these companies pursued?

3

Define accommodation theory. Using clothing as an example, explain how this theory would impact the ways in which companies market to different ethnic groups.

4

Define the three different types of reference group. Give examples of each of these groups as they relate to you.

5

What is the difference between normative and informational influence? Are some products more susceptible to one form of influence compared to the other? Provide examples.

6

In what ways can on religion impact on consumer behaviour?

7

Describe the two main types of consumer-related reference groups. Do you or anyone you know belong to any? How could membership in such a group impact your behaviour?

Exercise 1

You are a marketing intern at a publishing company. You have been given the task of developing a marketing plan for a new magazine targeted to a growing ethnic group in your country. How would you promote the new magazine? What would the actual product look like? Where would it be sold? How would you price it? Which consumer behaviour theories would you consider in developing your plan?

Endnotes

1
Selig Center for Economic Growth (2008) *The Multicultural Economy*

2
Hall, E.T. (1959) *The Silent Language*, New York: Doubleday

3
Peñaloza, L. 'Atravesando Fronteras/ Border Crossings: A Critical Ethnographic Exploration of the Consumer Acculturation of Mexican Immigrants'; *Journal of Consumer Research*, 21:1, June 1994

4
'Hostess Launches Line of Hispanic Snack Cakes', *Progressive Grocer,* 23 August 2005

5
'Gum ads played on stereotypes'; BBC News Online, 28 March 2007

6
Tomlinson, R. 'L'Oreal's Global Makeover How did a Brit from Liverpool turn an emblem of French chic into an international star? One brand at a time' *Fortune*, 22 September 2002

7
James, J. and Coady, E. 'Because they're worth it' *Time,* 26 January 2004

8
Zoepf, K. 'Bestseller in the Mideast: Barbie with a Prayer Mat' *The New York Times,* 22 September 2005

9
<www.premiermedia.org.uk>

10
Spindler, A. 16 March 1993, 'Gaultier Hits Home' *The New York Times*

11
Murphy, E. 'NASCAR not just for the boys anymore' *USA Today,* 2 July 2004

12
Leung, R. 'Undercover Marketing Uncovered: Hidden Cameras Capture Salespeople Secretly Pitching Products' 25 July 2004 <www.cbsnews.com>

13
Quelch, J. A. and Herman, H. 'McDonald's' *Harvard Business School Publishing,* 10 August 2007

14
Capell, K. 'A Golden Recipe for McDonald's Europe' *Businessweek,* 17 July 2008

15
Paul, D. 'The Muslim Big Mac' *The Daily Express,* 23 April 2007

Exercise 2

Interview five individuals regarding the groups that they would like to belong to or people they admire. Determine how these groups have impacted the interviewees' behaviour. Do these groups impact their purchasing, consumption, or disposal of these products in specific ways? How would you use this information as a marketer?

Factors such as social class, age and gender play an important role in the marketplace, and it is therefore important to monitor how these factors continue to evolve.

For example, the lines that traditionally divided social classes are becoming increasingly blurred. As the middle class in most developing countries continues to grow, many of these individuals now aspire to further climb the social class ladder. This opens up a huge market for luxury items and products made of higher quality components.

In addition to this, improvements in health care have led to populations in many different countries living longer. These seniors tend to have more disposable income than their younger counterparts and are a very viable market to target.

Finally, around the world women are becoming increasingly educated and are therefore earning more than in times gone by. For example, 25% of women in the United States earn more than their significant other; this makes them a market that cannot be ignored. For this reason, the market for products targeted to women has also grown exponentially over the past 25 years.

In this chapter, we will examine these factors and how they impact consumer behaviour and marketing strategies.

Nintendo Wii

In recent years Nintendo have done a great job of expanding the computer game market, which had previously been restricted to boys and young men. With health-conscious applications like *Wii Fit*, the addictive challenges of *Brain Training* and the gentle fun of *Animal Crossing* they have effectively made gaming appeal to almost every sector of society.

Most societies have some form of social class structure. This structure infers a certain amount of prestige or status to individuals based on their classification within the **hierarchy**. Members of each class share similar values and social status, and also tend to have shared patterns of consumer behaviour. An individual's social class can affect the leisure activities they take part in, the products and services they purchase, the organisations they join and their attitudes to certain products.

Before we examine the impact social class has on consumer behaviour, we need to examine how social class is determined. There are several factors that can be used to determine an individual's social class, including area of residence, possessions, family background, social interactions, inherited status and earned status. However, the three biggest indicators are education, occupation and income.

Running glossary

determinant
a factor which decisively affects the nature or outcome of something

hierarchy
a system in which members of an organisation or society are ranked according to relative status or authority

social mobility
moving from one social class to another, either upward or downward on the social class spectrum

A post-industrial society, being primarily a technical society, awards place less on the basis of inheritance or property ... than on education and skills.

Daniel Bell

Education

In broad terms, the more educated a person is the more likely they are to be employed in a profession that generates a lot of income and therefore to be of a higher status in society. Historically, gaining a university degree has had a big impact on an individual's future earning potential and is therefore seen as being the key to upward **social mobility**. However, several caveats have to be acknowledged – in most countries quality education is an expensive commodity meaning that children from poorer backgrounds may struggle to get access to good schools. Also, even when young adults from poorer backgrounds do gain a higher education they might not have the connections to take full advantage of their new-found qualifications. This is especially true in developing nations; but even in the United States only 7% of very low-income people attain a bachelor's degree by age 26.[1]

In response to this trend, schools such as Yale University and Harvard University are now offering free or reduced tuition to lower-income students who have been accepted. This programme provides more widespread support than needs-based scholarships and attempts to address the gap that still exists in access to education for the upper and lower classes.

Occupation

In western societies the greatest **determinant** of social class is occupation. Some occupations are afforded greater status than others simply because of the level of skill, training or education required to enter those particular professions. In many instances, individuals who share an occupation also possess similar goals, and purchase similar clothing, cars and leisure activities. For this reason, marketers often take occupation as the basis for segmenting markets and use this as a basis to sell their wares.

Social status rankings based on occupation tend to be based more on prestige than on objective criteria like income. Since this can be somewhat subjective, rankings of occupations based on societal prestige tend to vary from one country to another. In Western cultures many professions are routinely ranked higher than teachers in terms of status, except for university professors who typically rank fairly high on many status scales. However, in Eastern cultures, more prestige is frequently accorded to teachers than any other profession.

One reason why occupation is viewed as being a very influential determinant of social class is due to its relationship to income and education.

The Harris Poll – prestige ratings of occupations in the United States

The Harris Poll measured US public perceptions of 23 professions and occupations. The poll was conducted by telephone between 10th and 16th July 2007, by Harris Interactive® among a nationwide sample of 1,010 US adults. However, only about half of these adults were asked about each occupation. The interviewees were asked to respond to the following question: 'I am going to read off a number of different occupations. For each, would you tell me if you feel it is an occupation of very great prestige, considerable prestige, some prestige or hardly any prestige at all?'

Firefighter

Scientist

Teacher

Doctor

Military officer

Nurse

Police officer

Priest/Minister/Clergy

Farmer

Engineer

Member of Congress

Architect

Lawyer

Athlete

Business executive

Journalist

Union leader

Stockbroker

Entertainer

Accountant

Banker

Actor

Real estate agent/broker

Being born in the elite in the US gives you a constellation of privileges that very few people in the world have ever experienced. Being born poor in the US gives you disadvantages unlike anything in Western Europe and Japan and Canada.

David L. Levine

The Harris Poll – prestige ratings of occupations in the United States

% very great prestige	% considerable prestige	% some prestige	% hardly any prestige at all	% not sure/ refused
61	26	10	2	■
54	28	13	4	□
54	24	16	6	□
52	35	12	1	■
52	29	15	4	□
50	29	17	4	■
46	27	19	7	□
42	23	26	9	□
41	16	26	17	■
30	37	25	6	1
26	32	23	17	2
23	33	39	6	□
22	20	41	17	□
16	20	45	19	□
14	28	42	15	□
13	24	47	16	□
13	20	36	30	1
12	17	46	25	1
12	16	42	31	■
11	25	48	16	1
10	28	45	17	□
9	19	34	38	■
5	18	43	34	□

Base: all adults
■ No response
□ Less than 0.5%

Income

Marketers are very concerned with how income is distributed since this can enable them to target specific groups that can afford their products or services. Income can be used to predict what types of expensive purchases a consumer is likely to make – this is often dependent on what these purchases would symbolise to onlookers. However, income is not always a good indicator of social class. Several recent developments have weakened this link.

First, with more women joining the workforce, there are more dual-income families who are earning higher incomes but do not necessarily have the educational background or other characteristics that could lead to higher status. Second, many blue-collar workers can earn very high salaries with overtime and other benefits, but are not viewed as having higher standing.

Finally, through social promotion and union-negotiated increases in salary, some older workers naturally obtain higher salaries by virtue of being older. This does not lead to a concomitant change in social status.

The key point to take away from this discussion though is that even though the link between social class and income is not that strong, it is still one of the multiple factors that have some impact on how one's social standing is determined.

Social class and income as predictors of purchase behaviour

Even though income is not synonymous with social class, marketing researchers do agree that both social class and income can be useful in predicting purchase behaviour. For example, social class is a good predictor of purchases of low- to moderately priced goods that have some symbolic aspects that are derived from their usage, such as clothes and cosmetics. Equally, income is a good predictor of major expenditures that do not imply any status, such as major appliances. As marketers, we need to make use of both social class and income to predict the purchase of expensive products that have some symbolic significance and imply that the purchaser belongs to a certain social class, such as homes or automobiles.

Social class mobility

Social mobility is the process of moving either upward or downward on the social class spectrum. In the past, the American dream was linked to the notion of a poor person with high aspirations and a strong work ethic being able to achieve proportionate success in the United States. Recent research on mobility has shown that this is less likely to happen than we may think. Some economists believe that the mobility that many families experienced in the 1950s, 60s and 70s has now flattened or even declined.[2]

In spite of this, the aspirations of most groups to belong to the upper classes are still there, and this can significantly impact the way they behave in the marketplace.

These groups still purchase designer goods and more expensive products since it provides them with a greater association with their aspirant group. One company in New York City has seized this opportunity and is now renting luxury cars like Porches and Lamborghinis for a weekend. Typically, their clients are individuals who cannot afford to own these cars.

The structures of social class are dynamic and change over time. However, as our discussion on education illustrated, it is not an easy transition as social class determines access to educational opportunities, and thus limits an individual's prospects of moving up in social standing. So how does social class change?

Climbing up (and down) the social class ladder

In some cases, individuals move up from one social class to another, known as upward social mobility. Individuals can also move down in social class, although this only tends to happen during times of recession when individuals can lose their jobs and even their homes. As we've seen, upward mobility is often achieved through higher education and corresponding changes in occupation. However, recent studies in upward mobility have tracked consumers' income and other variables over decades and have found that there is not as much movement between classes as previously believed. It was once thought that individuals in a high social class would sustain that social advantage over another individual from the next lower social class for an average of three generations; this has now extended to almost five generations. There is some geographical variation, however, with social mobility being relatively high in the Scandinavian countries (Denmark, Sweden, Norway), at intermediate levels in Germany, and relatively low in the United Kingdom and the United States.[3] However, even in the UK and US social mobility is more fluid than in developing countries like Brazil, where escape from poverty is so difficult that members of the lower classes often have very little chance of moving upward in social class.[4]

How does social class affect consumption?

Social class affects consumer behaviour in different ways as many consumers are motivated by social class factors to acquire and consume certain products and services. Some of the ways in which social class can impact consumer behaviour include conspicuous consumption: the **trickle-down effect** and **status float** behaviour.

Conspicuous consumption

Conspicuous consumption refers to the purchase and subsequent conspicuous use of expensive products that clearly display one's social class. The *nouveau riche* (or newly wealthy) sometimes engage in conspicuous consumption so that others know that they have now 'arrived'. For example, some celebrities, like the American talk show host Jay Leno, have extensive automobile collections of very expensive modern or antique cars. This car collecting has now become a hobby of some wealthy consumers and they indulge themselves primarily to display their possessions to their peers.

Trickle-down effect

The trickle-down effect occurs when consumption patterns observed in the upper classes are copied by the lower classes. Consumers in the lower classes sometimes aspire to be like their wealthier counterparts and so they may consume similar products or services in order to 'live like the other half does'. Members of lower classes aspire to be wealthy and one way of feeling that this is being achieved is by purchasing products that the wealthy do, including cars, clothing and food.

Status float

Status float is effectively the reverse of the trickle-down effect, whereby consumers in the upper classes begin to copy purchase patterns and consumption behaviour previously seen in the lower classes. In many Western countries, wealthy suburban youth are now frequent purchasers of rap music and hip hop clothing. The hip hop phenomenon originated in the working class neighbourhoods in New York City.

Running glossary

status float
when consumers in the upper classes copy purchase patterns and consumption behaviour previously seen in the lower classes

trickle-down effect
when consumption patterns observed in the upper classes are copied by the lower classes

Affluent consumers continue to spend on luxury goods

While confidence in the US economy fluctuates, affluent consumers continue to maintain their luxury lifestyles. In 2008 affluent American consumers planned to spend significant amounts of money indulging in luxury goods and services.

In spite of the slowing economy, 84% of the very wealthy individuals (with a net worth of $30 million plus) said the current economic environment represented an investment opportunity, and that they would continue to spend more on luxury products and services and increase donations to charitable organisations than ever before.

In addition, 58% of individuals with a net worth of $10 to $30 million planned to increase spending on luxury goods as well.

Even though spending on luxury experiences declined slightly in 2006, spending on home and personal luxuries increased.[5] This reverses a trend from 2005 when spending on experiences rose, while home luxury spending declined over 2004. This trend of increased spending on luxuries continued though 2007 and, based on the survey, should have continued through 2008 and beyond.[6] Financial analysts predict that luxury sales will become a $1 trillion retail sector by 2010.

Targeting consumers who aspire to be like the upper class

Businesses are aware that some consumers copy the consumption patterns of the upper class and try to use that in marketing to these groups. They know that they would be willing to buy the brands that the upper classes purchase. For instance, luxury car companies sometimes manufacture a stripped down, more affordable vehicle for middle-class consumers. Mercedes-Benz sells a relatively low-price, lower-power C-Class line-up, starting with the four-cylinder C230. However, marketers must be careful when extending the brand like this since there could be brand dilution. Jaguar also used to sell a 2.5 X-Type, which was considerably cheaper than the other Jaguar models. These Jaguars were discontinued, though, when the company realised that their loyal customers who purchased the more expensive cars were complaining about Jaguar cheapening the brand.[7]

‹ What is social class?
Age and consumer identity
› How gender affects consumer behaviour

Consumers' needs and interests often change as they age. Younger consumers desire more active leisure activities than older consumers. They also tend to wear different clothing and purchase different types of foods than their senior counterparts. Older consumers tend to be more brand-loyal and can be more cautious when making purchases. Given these differences in age cohorts, marketers use age as a variable to place consumers into segments – or groups – to whom they could market their products and services.

Marketers have distinguished between the effect of chronological age (age effects) and also the effect of consumers' life experiences (cohort effects). Age effects occur naturally as we age and therefore demand different products and services. Consumers over 65 years old make greater use of healthcare services than other age groups; this is simply due to the impact of growing older. However, cohort effects occur when consumers are influenced by their experiences over the years, such as purchasing certain types of music or foods that they enjoyed while growing up. Their desire to consume these products does not have anything to do with their current chronological age, but is a consequence of their life experience.

Each different age group has distinct characteristics that make them attractive but challenging targets for marketers.

The senior market

One market with a great deal of potential is made up of older consumers. At the end of the Second World War there was a baby boom in several countries, especially those in Europe, Asia, and North America. During the period 1946–1966, over 76 million babies were born in the United States alone. With these groups aging, a prime marketing opportunity now exists for businesses to target the grey market (consumers aged 55 years and older).**8**

During the period 1987–2015 the population aged 54 years and younger is expected to grow by 20%, whereas the population aged 55 years and older is expected to grow by 60%. These consumers represent 50% of the discretionary income in the United States. They spend most of their money on exercise facilities, cruises and tourism, cosmetic surgery, skin treatments, education, and gifts for family members (especially grandchildren). This market has too much potential to be ignored.

Conspicuous consumption of valuable goods is a means of reputability to the gentleman of leisure.
Thorstein Veblen

Targeting seniors

Also known as the 'mature market', this segment has grown due to better health care in most developed countries, which has led to increased longevity. The market has become more financially viable since many of these seniors have saved over their lifetime and now have fewer debts to repay – hence they have much more disposable income than other age groups. In fact, in the United States, seniors control 70% of the disposable income, even though they make up only one third of the population. In addition to financial strength, growth in the senior market continues to outpace growth in the rest of the population. Between 2005 and 2030, the senior market will grow by 81%, while the remaining adult market (18–59 years of age) is expected to grow by approximately 7%.**9**

Seniors want the same goods and services as everyone else. However, they are more deliberate in their purchases and research most purchase decisions with more diligence than younger age groups. They are also a loyal group, so if a marketer attends to their needs then they are more than likely to stick with that company for a long time. The challenge lies in getting them to try your brand if it is new to them. The growing financial clout of this market means that fulfilling the needs and desires of older adults will be key to the success of many businesses in the coming years.

Marketing to seniors

Older consumers are motivated by several different values. Two of the most important are independence and connectedness. Even though they like to feel self-sufficient, they still like to remain in touch with their families and loved ones. Ads should highlight self-sufficiency and youth. Yet, ads that illustrate ties to family and friends will also be popular. Older consumers also do not like to be reminded that they are old. The editors of the *AARP (American Association of Retired Persons) Magazine* reject about a third of all ads companies submit to them because they portray seniors in a negative light. Companies need to recognise that older consumers might not feel their chronological age, so if they are targeted with images of elderly consumers who are not energetic, this might lead them to have negative feelings towards the brand.

‹ What is social class?
Age and consumer identity
› How gender affects consumer behaviour

Marketing to teens

The teen market is very attractive to marketers; this is partly due simply to its size. In the United Kingdom, 18% of the population is 14 years old or younger. In the United States, the group is 21% of the population; in China it is 25%; and in India it is as high as 33%.[10]

Thus, the size of the global market offers a substantial opportunity for marketers and represents great future potential. If marketers can instil brand loyalty at this early stage then they may have a lifetime of loyal customers. The teen market is not only large in terms of numbers; it also wields a lot of buying power. It is estimated that in 2006 American teens spent $195 billion. Their money comes primarily from part-time jobs and parents. Teenagers spend their money on clothes, eating out, cars, movies, phones and small electronics. So how do marketers reach these teens in the future? The answer may lie with the Internet – 65% of teens have reported setting up a social networking personal page.

Also, as today's teens tend to be more technically proficient than their parents, they tend to have a great deal of influence on household decisions for purchases of electronics and computer peripherals.

Running glossary

age compression
a controversial marketing strategy in which products and attitudes normally associated with adults and older teenagers are promoted to children and young teens

A little girl getting a manicure is no big deal. It's the idea of this becoming routine and starting so early – that's what makes it harmful. There's a graduation to makeup and thong parties, so that girls look like they're 13 when they're 7 and like they're 20 when they're 13. It's important for people to take it seriously.
Jean Kilbourne[11]

The 'tween' market

The so-called 'tween' market covers children aged seven to 14 years old. These young consumers are increasingly becoming the target of businesses that formerly marketed to older teens and adults. This marketing effort is driven by a phenomenon called '**age compression**'. Children are maturing earlier; they are exposed to outside influences at a much younger age. These children are now becoming computer literate earlier than in past years and are given greater independence to make their own buying decisions. However, marketing to 'tweens' is a challenging venture.

This group is even more fickle and less brand-loyal than older teens. Their sense of style, though very sharp, is constantly shifting. This makes the tween market a difficult, albeit rewarding, market to target.[12] Tweens tend to imitate looks that they see older teens wearing, yet they still want to call it their own. This provides manufacturers the opportunity to alter teen fashions and accessories to give them a younger look – especially one that is more palatable to parents.

Tweens are also becoming more socially conscious. They want to know that firms do not test on animals and some become vegetarians or vegans at an early age. Bonne Bell, a firm that markets products to tweens, reports having received thank you letters from tweens for the company's environmentally friendly practices.

Manufacturers who are aware of the idiosyncrasies and ever-changing tastes of this lucrative market can earn tremendous rewards from targeting tweens. But there are risks involved in targeting very young consumers: the first danger is that products and styles will very quickly go out of fashion amongst this most fickle of groups. Secondly, marketers run the risk of alienating parents (who of course typically supply the finances for their children's purchases). For example, clothing stores like Victoria's Secret and Abercrombie & Fitch recently received some negative publicity by targeting this age group. Abercrombie & Fitch received the brunt of the criticism when they tried to market thong underwear to tweens.

〈 Age and consumer identity
How gender affects consumer behaviour
〉 Case study: What women want

When targeting consumers, marketers must be cognizant of the differences between men and women. Men and women respond differently to marketing stimuli. This can be traced back to their historical societal roles.

Sixty years ago male and female roles were very distinct; men were the primary bread-winners and society expected them to be strong and assertive. Men had to master their emotions and their environment. They were ruled by **agentic goals**. These goals emphasise dominance and assertiveness.

Women were supposed to be the more caring members of society, who were in touch with their feelings. They were expected to be concerned with the group dynamic, especially within their families, and making sure everyone was feeling fine. At that time, women were governed by **communal goals**, focusing on harmony and establishing relationships.

Blurring the lines

Since the 1950s, these distinctions have become more and more blurred – with women adopting more competitive, 'agentic' attitudes as they adapt to traditionally male-dominated work environments. Equally, the male societal role has changed significantly in most societies; as their wives become more independent and work more outside the home, men have taken on greater responsibility for household duties and child rearing. This involves taking on some 'communal' goals.

However, even though their roles are changing and both men and women are assuming roles that were traditionally considered roles for the opposite gender, differences still exist in how they behave as consumers.

When targeting men, marketers must present information that men respond to more positively. Usually, this means the information must be personally relevant. As dictated by agentic goals, men are very sensitive to information that is personally relevant. They like to view commercials that relate to products and services for themselves. On the other hand, women are interested in marketing communications that are relevant to both themselves and their family or close friends. Thus, the communal goals still come into play for females.

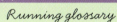

Targeting women

Over 80% of the buying decisions in US households are made by women. They are the principal decision makers for most families. Women now make decisions about products that were traditionally the domain of the males in the household. For example, women are buying the majority of all consumer-electronics and home-improvement goods today.

Marketers are cashing in on the increasing role of women in traditionally male-dominated markets. For example, Home Depot, Sears and Lowe's are targeting women by hosting special home improvement classes for women. 80% of women surveyed by Home Depot stated that working with their own tools makes them feel more independent.[13] Home Depot has therefore increased its focus on product innovation and in-store environment, making its environment and products more female-friendly.

In addition, manufacturers like Barbara K are responding to this opportunity and have created a tool line specifically targeted to women. Barbara K's 30-piece tool kit is sold in home improvement and variety stores. These tools are not only better looking but are also made for a woman's size and strength. They weigh a little less than regular tools, and the grips are sized to better fit a woman's hand.[14]

Running glossary

agentic goals
goals that emphasise dominance and assertiveness

communal goals
goals that stress harmony and establishing relationships

Background

Until relatively recently, the needs of female customers were of very little concern to retailers and producers. Products were developed and marketed in a supposedly gender-neutral way – but in effect this meant that they were targeted to male needs. The first voice recognition systems were a classic example of this as they were developed without consideration of female vocal patterns. As Martina Schraudner, of the Munich-based market research firm Fraunhofer-Gesellschaft, noted: 'They didn't recognise any female voices, since the developers hadn't taken their speech patterns into account'. The earliest airbags were even more frightening because, once again, male developers apparently took themselves as the standard: 'Since the ergonomic factor of size was initially neglected, the first airbags were a life-threatening safety risk for women and children', says Schraudner.[15]

However, as women around the world have gained increasing access to tertiary education, higher paid jobs, and disposable income, producers, marketers and retailers have begun to take more notice of their needs.

Designing for women

Consulting firm A.T. Kearney estimates that women determine 80% of consumption, purchase 60% of all cars and own 40% of all stocks. Companies worldwide are therefore now caught in a 'pink' marketing wave, with the car industry leading the way, and not just in their marketing campaigns. Many companies are finally considering women's needs at the design stage; for example, DaimlerChrysler's engineers in Stuttgart have included features such as handbag storage and making seatbelts cleavage-friendly. They have also added a heating ventilation system in some models that warms the necks of drivers, apparently a female-friendly feature. These small but convenient innovations can pay significant commercial dividends; for example, when General Motors introduced female-friendly features – like the electric hatchback for its SRX model Cadillac – it was able to increase the proportion of female buyers from 40% to 54%.

Women are a growing market force we have to address. This development is essential to our survival, according to industry estimates, the share of women who own cars will rise from 30% to 50% over the next 20 years.

Thomas Weber, DaimlerChrysler

London   Manchester   Brighton   Tokyo   Sydney   www.boxfresh.co.uk

Boxfresh – 'streetwear' fashion
This advert for urban 'streetwear'
clothing brand Boxfresh challenges
expectations of the target market.

< How gender affects consumer behaviour
Case study / What women want
> Questions and exercises

Girlfriend groups

Marketers have developed innovative ways of gathering data on women's needs. A new trend is known as 'girlfriend groups'.[16] Marketers hire one female shopper to recruit several of her girlfriends and they meet for an evening of fun, food, and research. Once they get to their friend's house, they meet researchers who ask them questions about brands and products. These sessions are less formal than focus groups and tend to get more honest and forthcoming results. In a typical focus group setting, women tend to be more guarded, but in girlfriend groups, they let their hair, and their guard, down. These research results have proven to be useful for all types of industries including health care and beauty products.

Around the globe, more companies have realised that they overlook women at their own financial peril. Such companies are realigning their marketing and design practices, and learning to court an increasingly female-centric consumer base that boasts more financial muscle and purchasing independence than ever before.

Question 1
In addition to the fact that women have increased purchasing power, are there any other reasons why firms should target women?

Question 2
Identify three products that are being sold to both men and women but are designed primarily for men. How would you refine one of these products to make it more appealing to women (without alienating the male customer base)?

Question 3
Girlfriend groups have proven to be an effective way of collecting information about women. What other types of research methods might work especially well with women? Why?

K2 Skis

US ski manufacturer K2 was able to increase ski sales to women by 25% within one year after developing a new model designed for women's low centre of gravity.

Discussion questions

1

What are the determinants of social class?

2

What are the different ways in which social class can affect consumer behaviour? Provide specific examples of products or services.

3

Marketers have identified two different effects of age on consumer behaviour – age and cohort effects. Define each and explain how these two effects differ.

4

What are upward and downward mobility? Which factors could lead to each occurring?

5

Men and women are motivated by different types of goals. Describe these goals and explain how they could impact on how consumers behave in the marketplace.

Exercise 1

Locate two different websites that sell similar products, one that targets the upper class and one that targets the lower class. How do these websites differ in appearance and in their offerings? Do they differ in any other ways? What does this tell you about how marketers target the different social classes?

Exercise 2

Interview three teens and three seniors (people over 55 years of age). Determine what types of goods and services they purchase on a regular basis. What accounts for most of their spending? What items would they like to buy if money were no object? Do these two groups differ in significant ways?

Endnotes

1
Anyon, J. and Green, K. 'No Child Left Behind as an Anti-Poverty Measure' *Teacher Education Quarterly,* Spring 2007

2
Tom Hertz (2006) 'Understanding Mobility in America', Center for American Progress, 26 April 2006

3
Corak, M. (ed.) *Generational Income Mobility in North America and Europe*, Cambridge, Cambridge University Press, December 2004

4
Scott, J. and Leonhardt, D. 'Class in America: Shadowy Lines that Still Divide' *The New York Times,* 15 May 2005

5
'In 2007 luxury consumer spending shifts' *Businesswire,* 6 June 2007

6
'The Elite Traveler Affluent Consumer Survey' *Elite Traveler,* January 2008

7
Healey, J. 'Cheapest Jags get kicked to the curb' *USA Today,* 28 May 2005

8
Matt Rosenberg (2009) 'Baby Boom: The Population Baby Boom of 1946–1964 in the United States', About.com, 26 March 2009

9
The 2008 Statistical Abstract, US Census Bureau

10
Parmar, A. 'Global Youth United' *Marketing News,* 28 October 2002

11
Puente, M. 'From the Sandbox to the Spa' *USA Today,* 1 August 2006

12
O'Donnell, J. 'As Kids get Savvy, Marketers move down the age scale' *USA Today,* 13 April 2007

13
Tsao, A. 'Retooling Home Improvement' *Businessweek,* 14 February 2005

14
'Marketing to Women', Special Report, *Businessweek,* 14 February 2005

15
Bonstein, J. 'The Challenge of Marketing to Women' *Businessweek,* 15 May 2007

16
Meece, M. 'What do Women want? Just ask.' *The New York Times,* 29 October 2006

Exercise 3

Think of a product or service targeted primarily to women that you believe could be successful if targeted to men. Create a brief marketing plan for this product or service. What would it look like? Would it be any different now that you are selling it to men? Where would you sell it? How would you price it? How would you advertise it? In what media? What would the ads look like?

Going organic

Philadelphia cream cheese has been around since 1872, when it was first made in a small New York dairy. Kraft now sells it in 80 countries around the world, with 'light' and 'extra light' versions for the diet market and now an organic option for a new group of specialist consumers. Most consumers who purchase organic foods are motivated by strongly held beliefs about their health.

Consumers use products and services for a reason; some are easy to articulate and others are not. Some satisfy very basic physiological needs such as thirst or hunger, while others satisfy more complex, psychological needs such as self-fulfilment. This chapter examines the forces that drive individuals to consume the products they do – to choose one product over another.

On the most basic level, the forces that drive people to buy and consume products are usually easy to identify – for instance, a consumer might purchase bottled water simply because they are thirsty. However, even the choice of basic food products can still be tied to deeply held beliefs as to what is appropriate or desirable. Consider those consumers who choose to only purchase organic foods; they are often driven by beliefs about health, the environment and food safety. In some instances, these beliefs trigger emotional responses that lead to a deep commitment to certain relevant products. The theories of motivation, perception and attitude help us to understand why consumers such as these do the things they do.

Motivation refers to the inner state of arousal that leads people to behave the way they do. It occurs when a need is aroused within the consumer that they have to satisfy. If that need, is not satisfied then the consumer will undergo a certain amount of tension – the greater the need the more intense is the state of tension. This drives the consumer to engage in relevant activity to achieve their goal and satisfy the need.

Many factors can affect motivation, including personal relevance, perceived risks and a consumer's personal values. The outcomes of high motivation include goal-relevant behaviour, high-effort information processing and high levels of involvement. Let's return to our organic food example to see this in action.

The effects of high motivation

More and more consumers are making a commitment to healthy living and environmental responsibility. These consumers are therefore highly motivated to search for and purchase foods that support this commitment – affecting everything from the milk and cheese that they purchase to the meat that they eat.

This trend in healthy eating has been growing worldwide over the past decade. In the UK, despite the fact that organic products account for little more than 1% of overall food and drink sales, there is no doubt that these products have joined the mainstream. Indeed, organic products are now available from all the major grocery brands, and the majority of households buy organic food, even if some are only doing so very occasionally.

This has led to the organic food market experiencing double-digit growth in the United Kingdom. Fruit and vegetables had sales of £442 million in 2005, making up 37% of the total market. But the biggest rise is in meat and poultry sales – up nearly 150% between 2000 and 2005. This growth is expected to continue with sales projected to reach £2 billion by 2010. Consumer health and environmental concerns have had a very real impact on the grocery market.[1]

People often say that motivation doesn't last. Well, neither does bathing – that's why we recommend it daily.

Zig Ziglar

Motivation leads to involvement

Some people can get very attached to products. When a consumer is motivated to achieve a goal, they will engage in different activities that are aimed towards achieving that goal. However, not everyone will be attached to a specific product (or brand) to the same extent. Some individuals have demonstrated unwavering loyalty towards one brand compared to others. For example, as we'll see in the case study on page 100, Harley-Davidson riders tend to be highly involved with the brand. So much so that Harley riders would not even consider riding on a different brand of motorcycle. Some Harley customers have even been known to get tattoos of the Harley logo.

The motivation for all personal behaviour is to produce a sense of 'feel good', a sense of inner peace and well being. To expect a person to go against his desire to feel good or as good as he can feel under any momentary condition is illogical and irrational. In the observation of human behaviour, one will notice every human act is a response to a personal need.

Sidney Madwed

Goals

When consumers are highly motivated their behaviour becomes more goal-oriented. They tend to perform actions that make it more likely for them to achieve their goals. For example, if you are motivated to purchase a new laptop, you might go to different stores to examine the different laptops on the market; you may also visit websites to read relevant reviews and compare prices. You would perform these actions since this would lead you to achieving your goal of owning a laptop that you like.

Consumers usually have two types of goal. The first type is a **generic** goal – something that will fulfil a consumer's need. For instance, if a consumer states that he is hungry and he wants to eat a meal, he has stated a generic goal. However, if of all of the meal options open to him he states that he wants a McDonald's hamburger, that is a product-specific goal. This type of goal is of major concern to marketers since these goals determine the types of products and brands that consumers choose.

Goal-relevant behaviour

The *Live Earth Concert* series has had worldwide success in promoting environmentally friendly causes. Assume that you are a consumer who purchases primarily organically grown food due to your environmental concerns. If you discover that your favourite artist is performing at the concert you would be highly motivated to purchase tickets for the concert since there are two needs that would be satisfied if you attend the concert – you would be supporting environmentally friendly causes and you would be able to see your favourite artist. Therefore, you would engage in activities to achieve this goal, including waiting in long lines to purchase tickets and setting aside the time to attend the day-long concert.

Motivation is the art of getting people to do what you want them to do because they want to.
Dwight David Eisenhower

Consumer involvement

In addition to encouraging goal-relevant behaviour, motivation leads to a **psychological** state called **involvement**. This is the relevance of an object to a person based on the individual's needs and values. The more motivated a consumer is, the more likely they are to become highly involved with the product, service or brand. As involvement increases, individuals become more likely to devote a greater amount of attention to searching for information about the product or service. They are also likely to pay more attention to advertising about the object and also to process information about it.

Motivation is what gets you started. Habit is what keeps you going.
Jim Rohn

Running glossary

generic
characteristic of or relating to a class or group of things; not specific

involvement
the relevance of an object to a person based on the individual's needs and values

psychological
of, affecting, or arising in, the mind: related to the mental and emotional state of the person

Consumer perception

Perception is defined as: 'the process by which consumers select, organise and interpret stimuli to create a coherent and meaningful picture of the world around them'.[2]

This process occurs automatically and helps us make sense of the world. Before we perceive objects, though, we must be exposed to them, and then pay attention to them. The sequence from exposure to attention to perception is played out many times during our daily lives.

From exposure to perception

Exposure refers to the process whereby a consumer comes into contact with marketing stimuli such as brand names, commercials, jingles and billboards. Exposure is very important since this begins the process towards final purchase and consumption of the product. Research has shown that consumers are more likely to approach and select a brand that has an exposure advantage over its competitors. In *Advertising Repetition: A Critical Review of Wear-in and Wear-out*[3] (1989), Pechman and Stewart suggest that attitudes toward advertising are related to the number of exposures to advertising. In this way, unfamiliar brands and advertising messages will not receive as favourable a response as their better-known competitors.

The amount of exposure a company's product receives is impacted by several factors. It could be influenced by how an ad is placed in a newspaper or magazine – ads that are placed on the back cover usually receive a great deal of exposure, and television commercials that are shown at the beginning or at the end of a commercial block receive more exposure than those in the interim. Product distribution also impacts exposure. Brands that are widely distributed receive more exposure than other brands. A brand such as Coca-Cola is so widely distributed that it has much better brand recognition than its competitors.

The 'now' consumer is accessing content at home, at work, at the mall, during their commute – on every device imaginable. Advertising packages that succeed in combining those distribution outlets to maximize the client's exposure and reach the consumer on multiple touch points are the ones that will succeed.

Greg D'Alba

Attention

No matter how much exposure a brand receives, this is not enough to lead to purchase and consumption. A certain amount of attention must be paid to the stimulus to which a customer is exposed in order for it to be perceived. Attention is the process by which you devote some of your mental resources to a stimulus. Marketers need to understand the characteristics of attention since this can have a direct impact on their brand's success. Attention is selective – we cannot pay full attention to multiple stimuli at the same time.

For example, if you want to purchase a gift for your partner a possible option might be a bottle of perfume or cologne. While shopping you may be exposed to many different brands, ads, displays, smells, and also many other gift options competing for your attention and, subsequently, your purchase. As a consumer, you must sift through all of the competing stimuli and determine to which you would like to devote your processing effort. In this case anything to do with perfume or cologne would 'leap out' while less relevant information is relegated to the background.

Cutting through the clutter

Given that consumers are exposed to a multitude of ads on a daily basis, marketers go to great lengths to grab their attention and cut through the clutter. For example, on the London Tube and New York City Subway companies often purchase sufficient space to display several related ads in sequence. This leads to the consumer being exposed to many ads for the same product all in the same venue. The same strategy is used in many airports – companies purchase all of the ad space on either side of a moving walkway and have a captive audience to whom they can display their goods or services.

Appealing to the senses

Once the consumer has been exposed to a stimulus, and devoted some attention to it, they are then ready to perceive it. In other words, the stimulus is picked up by one of their five senses – sight, hearing, taste, touch or smell. Over the years, marketers have targeted all of these senses in their attempts to reach consumers. However, the senses of vision and smell have played the biggest roles in efforts to enhance perception.

Vision

Several factors influence how we perceive visual stimuli. Marketers use a product's size, styling and colour to influence how it is perceived by consumers. One example is the Jitterbug mobile phone, launched in 2006. At first glance this phone appears bulky and the keys seem too large. All aspects of the phone are bigger than usual – but this is all by design. This phone is targeted primarily to seniors who appreciate these attributes. The phone also has a simple user interface and is curved to fit in the palm of the hand to further appeal to the older target market.[4]

Colour can also be hugely important to consumer perception as it can influence mood and attitude; it is often the last reason to buy a product, but it's the first thing a consumer sees. Whereas colours such as red lead to arousal, blue tends to have a calming influence. Products presented against a red background are less liked than products presented against a blue background. The preference for blue is somewhat global; **cross-cultural** studies have shown a consistent preference for blue in Eastern as well as Western countries.[5] Indeed, American Express even named one of its credit cards the Blue Card after research showed that the colour led to feelings of optimism.

Running glossary

cross-cultural
relating to different cultures or comparison between them

prototype
a first or preliminary version of a device or vehicle from which other forms are developed

Smell

Scents can have a positive or negative impact on an individual's emotions. Marketers are very interested in the impact of positive odours on product evaluations and consumer memory. One study examined consumers who were exposed to familiar and unfamiliar brand names in either a pleasantly scented or unscented environment. A computer recorded how much time they took to evaluate each brand. When they were exposed to pleasant scents, they evaluated brands more positively – especially for brands that they had not heard of before. Consumers also displayed better memory for these unfamiliar brand names when exposed to a pleasant scent.[6]

Due to findings such as these, the business of 'scent marketing' has been growing and marketers are coming up with different ways to combine scents with products and retail environments. ScentAndrea is a particularly strong example. They make a handful of innocuous looking products such as mirrors, coffee machines and fans, all outfitted with scent distributors. The idea is to surreptitiously add appealing aromas to a retail environment, making you think of fresh-baked pie, for instance, as you approach the outskirts of a grocery store's bakery area.

The company also makes an odour-emitting mouse to add a similar olfactory dimension to your Internet shopping experience. Available scents range from food aromas such as 'garlic butter' and 'baking cinnamon rolls' to environmental choices like 'redwood forest' and 'oily machinery'.

Another company, DigiScents, unveiled the iSmell in 2001. This shark-fin-shaped apparatus plugged into the USB port of a computer and wafted appropriate scents as you surfed smell-enabled websites – perfume as you were browsing the Chanel website, for example. The product did not move much beyond the **prototype** stage, however, since sceptical users did not believe that the device could provide accurate scents. The jury is still out on the ScentAndrea mouse, but their products for retail environments have been well accepted thus far.[7]

Consumer attitudes

Marketers define attitude as a general, lasting evaluation of an attitude object. An attitude object is any person, object, advertisement or issue to which you have an attitude. An attitude endures over time and it must apply to many different situations and not to a momentary event. For instance, if someone feels negatively about wine only when they see teenagers drinking, and feels positively about it on all other occasions, then they would not be described as having a negative attitude towards wine. It is important for marketers to understand how attitudes are formed and how they could be influenced since this could help them influence consumers' decisions.

Running glossary

affective component
consumer's emotions about the attitude object

cognitive component
a consumer's cognitions, thoughts and beliefs about the attitude object

conative component
the likelihood that the consumer will perform an action

The tri-component model of attitudes

Most marketers agree that attitudes have three components: **cognitive** (what consumers think), **affective** (what consumers feel) and **conative** (what consumers do). Consumers decide which adverts to view, which stores to visit, which products they like and what to purchase all based on their attitudes.

The thinking component of attitude consists of a consumer's cognitions: their thoughts and beliefs about the attitude object. For example, if you were to list the different attributes that you assign to the MacBook Air (such as lightweight) these would make up the 'thinking' component of your attitude towards this product.

The feeling or 'affective' component of a consumer's attitude is evaluative in nature; it captures a consumer's overall assessment of the item in question. This assessment could be favourable or unfavourable.

The doing component deals with the likelihood that the consumer will perform an action (that is purchase a product or service). In determining what consumers will do, marketers collect data about the consumer's intention to buy. It must be noted that many factors can impact on whether a consumer eventually acts on their intention; they may not, for example, have the money available.

The foundations of attitudes

Some attitudes are based on researched information. So, if you are planning a trip to the movies and need to decide on which film to see, you might read published reviews or ask friends for recommendations. The information you collect would serve as the basis for forming your attitude towards the movie, even before you see it. A second approach proposes that attitude is based on 'affect' or feelings. We establish our attitudes to some products by experiencing them. This generally occurs for inexpensive products, for example if you want to find out if you like Vanilla Coca-Cola, the simplest way is to buy it, try it and decide.

Although attitude alone may not predict behaviour, it is still a powerful concept in marketing. Unsurprisingly, marketers are particularly interested in changing attitudes; if we are able to influence consumers' attitudes then we can directly impact sales.

Two groups of variables have been shown to influence the impact of communication on consumer attitudes. First, source credibility and attractiveness is important to changing attitudes. If the information is supplied by someone that the consumer trusts and respects, then the message that they are conveying is far more likely to be given credence.

For this reason, many marketing messages are presented by persons with expertise of some sort – such as a dentist extolling the virtues of Colgate toothpaste. As consumers, we must determine how believable the source is. Sources are generally credible when they possess one or more of the following: trustworthiness, expertise and/or status.

The second group of variables is related to the message itself. It includes: perceptual aspects of the advert such as visual elements or vividness; learning and memory aspects such as repetition; one- versus two-sided arguments, or comparative advertising; and affective aspects such as emotional, sex, humour and fear appeals.

Spokesperson credibility

When a message is complex, or when there is a good match between product and endorser, the spokesperson is more believable. However, there are factors that could negatively impact the spokesperson's credibility. The first is overexposure and could occur when a spokesperson endorses too many products. At one stage in his career, basketball player Michael Jordan endorsed approximately 37 products. He was in great danger of being overexposed; this would have reduced the effectiveness of ads in which Jordan was the spokesperson.

< Consumer attitudes
Case study / **The Harley-Davidson community**
> Questions and exercises

Background

In 1983, Harley-Davidson established the Harley Owners Group (H.O.G.) in the United States. This group was established because of the developing interest of Harley owners in participating in organised activities with other Harley enthusiasts. Membership grew rapidly and in the 1990s, H.O.G. went international, hosting the first official European H.O.G. Rally in Cheltenham, England. Membership continued to grow around the world in Europe and Asia, including countries such as Singapore and Malaysia. The goal of the H.O.G. was to enhance the level of involvement that Harley riders felt towards the Harley brand and their main product: the Harley motorcycle. Membership of H.O.G brought with it many benefits, including access to the company's *HOG® Magazine*, insurance, roadside assistance and Harley rentals at several locations worldwide. However, one of the major events established to generate enthusiasm for the brand and stimulate consumer involvement was the Posse Ride.

The Harley-Davidson Posse Ride

In order to increase their riders' level of involvement with their products, and enhance brand loyalty, Harley began promoting destination rallies. Harley owners would attend a 'Homecoming' event held in Milwaukee, Wisconsin, where the Harley headquarters is located, as well as local and regional rallies. These rallies would bring together thousands of Harley enthusiasts and would link Harley riders to a wider Harley community. This created a sense of togetherness that engendered a greater appreciation for the Harley brand.

However, these destination rallies proved very expensive to administer and required up to 100 Harley employees to assist with the smooth running of the events. The company therefore decided to adopt the concept of 'touring rallies'. These are rallies that take the form of a long-distance bike ride. They emphasise actually riding the Harley and provide a sense of camaraderie that the stationary rallies do not. Riders go through several checkpoints and receive documentation proving that they have completed the different stages of the ride. They are hosted by Harley dealers who are eager to connect with Harley riders and showcase their businesses in the local media. The rallies also often include a theme based on the route that the tour takes. For example, the 'Blues Cruise' focused on stops that highlighted American musical history.[8]

A classic Harley
The Posse Rides create enhanced brand loyalty by offering their customers an opportunity to show off their bikes and feel a sense of camaraderie with fellow enthusiasts.

〈 Consumer attitudes
Case study / The Harley-Davidson community
〉 Questions and exercises

Enhancing involvement with the Harley brand

The Posse Ride is now steeped in tradition and rituals. At the beginning of the tour, riders take a 'Posse Oath' regarding their participation in the ride (including a 'no whining' clause). They are given a 'passport' which is stamped every time they complete a stage of the ride. They also participate in several other tour activities with the other members often entertaining each other with stories about the adventures they've had with their Harleys. These activities help the ride participants build a stronger bond with the Harley community and also increase their sense of identification with the Harley brand.

Groups like the Harley Owners' Group are called brand communities. They are made up of consumers who share similar values and goals that relate to a particular brand. Some such brands, like Harley, become a cultural phenomenon and are associated with a specific lifestyle. The brand then makes a statement about the owner; Harley owners are considered rebellious and carefree.

Harley-Davidson has decided to put more resources into the touring rallies since they are a valuable opportunity to get close to their main consumers. They can listen to their consumers' concerns and also get ideas on how to improve their motorcycles and the attendant services. For the rider, membership in the brand community only serves to strengthen their relationship with the brand. This in turn leads to increased involvement and a more positive attitude towards Harley.

The ultimate brand loyalty

A well-developed brand can inspire incredible levels of loyalty and consumer identification.

Question 1
Do you believe brand communities like Harley-Davidson result in greater involvement with the brand?

Question 2
What elements of the Posse Ride do you believe enhance the meaning of the brand for the riders?

Question 3
Should Harley-Davidson get more involved in the ride or would that dilute the ride's meaning to the participants?

Question 4
In addition to experiences such as the Posse Ride, what other ways could Harley increase involvement in the brand?

Questions and exercises

>

Discussion questions

1

What is motivation and what are the outcomes of motivation?

2

What is involvement? How would higher levels of involvement in a product category influence a consumer's behaviour when purchasing products within that category?

3

The amount of exposure a brand receives is essential to its success in the marketplace. What factors influence the amount of exposure received by a brand?

4

Describe the different elements of the tri-component model of attitudes.

5

Marketers have targeted all of our senses in their attempts to reach consumers. Can you give any personal examples of how marketers have used vision, smell and colour to enhance your perception of their offerings?

6

What strategies can marketers use to attract consumers' attention? Are any of these strategies more effective than the others? Why, or why not?

7

What are the characteristics of attention? How could these characteristics affect how consumers behave?

Exercise 1

Charles is a loyal fan of Arsenal Football Club and has a high level of involvement with that club. He attends every home game and most away games. If you were the marketing manager at Arsenal, how would you design a strategy for Charles? Would that strategy be different from a strategy for a casual Arsenal supporter who only attends home games three times during each season and watches most of the other games on television? Would there be differences in the product, promotion, pricing or distribution strategies?

Exercise 2

Visit a retail store near you. Using consumer behaviour theory, describe the strategies used at the store entrance and in the store to attract your attention. How could the store management improve on their attempts to attract attention?

Exercise 3

Select three different print magazine advertisements. Rate your overall attitude towards each ad. What elements of the source (such as the spokesperson or company) or message (such as the visual elements, humour or fear appeals) influence your attitude towards each ad? If your attitude to any of the ads is not very positive, what could a marketer change in order to make your attitude more positive?

Endnotes

1
'Organic Food Sales Soar in the United Kingdom' *Quick Frozen Foods International,* 1 January 2006

2
Lindsay, P. and Norman, D. A. (1977) *Human Information Processing: An Introduction to Psychology,* New York, Academic Press

3
Pechman, C. and Stewart, D. W. (1988) 'Advertising Repetition: A Critical Review of Wear-in and Wear-out. In Leigh, J. H. and C. R. Martin Jr. (Eds.), *Current Issues and Research in Advertising* pp. 285–289, Ann Arbor, MI: University of Michigan

4
Pogue, D. 'Some phones are just, well phones' *The New York Times,* 28 September 2006

5
Chattopadhyay, A., Darke, P. and Gorn, G. (2008) 'Roses are Red and Violets are Blue – Everywhere? Cultural and Universals in Color Preference and Choice Among Consumers and Marketing Managers', Sauder School of Business Working Paper

6
Morrin, M. and Ratneshwar, S. (2000) 'The Impact of Ambient Scent on Evaluation, Attention, and Memory for Familiar and Unfamiliar Brands'; *Journal of Business Research,* pp. 157–165

7
Becker, D. 'The Sweet Smell of Marketing' *Wired,* 7 November 2006

8
Fournier, S. 'Building Brand Community on the Harley Davidson Posse Ride' Harvard Business School Publishing, 1 November 2000

When a consumer makes a decision, they usually make use of the information already stored in their memory. This information tends to be structured and organised using associations between the various pieces of information. These linkages enable the consumer to recall information from their 'knowledge base' when required to do so. The manner in which this knowledge is encoded, organised and stored has a direct impact on consumers' decision making.

Knowledge is generally comprised of associations we link to different objects – these could be physical attributes or abstract ideas and concepts. These associations have certain characteristics. They can be salient, unique, or favourable/unfavourable.

To put this into context, think of the Kellogg's Frosted Flakes (or Frosties) brand of breakfast cereal. Certain associations should spring to mind, such as 'crunchy' and 'ice-cold milk'. These are the more salient associations linked to the brand. Other thoughts that come to mind are unique and can only be associated with this brand, like 'Tony the Tiger'. Finally some associations are favourable (convenient and tasty) or negative (sugary). Companies like Kellogg's work hard at eliminating the negative associations and promoting the positive and salient associations that lead to their brands holding a positive and prominent place in their consumers' minds.

Tony the Tiger – 'They're grrreat!'
Tony the Tiger is uniquely associated with Frosted Flakes (Frosties) cereal and has been helping consumers easily distinguish it from competing brands since 1952.

What is knowledge?

Knowledge is the outcome of the collection and assimilation of information through learning. All of the information that we have learned about products, brands, product usage and so on, comprise our knowledge base. Consumers group this information together in a manner that makes sense to them. So, similar items might be stored together. This system of information organisation and storage is known as the consumer's **knowledge structure**. Consumer knowledge is important to marketers since consumers use their prior knowledge to categorise or label products. **Categorisation** is the process of placing a mental 'label' on a product, based on available information.

Running glossary

categorisation
the process of placing a product or brand in a particular class or group

knowledge structure
how information is organised and stored

We have a hunger of the mind which asks for knowledge of all around us, and the more we gain, the more is our desire; the more we see, the more we are capable of seeing.
Maria Mitchell

Remembering the good old days

Before anyone wore Air Jordans, there were Chuck Taylor All Stars. These shoes were named for Charles Taylor, a basketball star who played with several professional basketball teams in the 1920s. He worked with the Converse Rubber Shoe Co. to improve the sneaker and endorsed the shoe that eventually bore his name. The high-top shoe with a canvas upper and a rubber sole was a hit. People liked the fit and the cost. Consumers over the years have bought millions of the Converse Chuck Taylor shoes. 'It wasn't a style', said 71-year-old John Franchville of Ocala, who has been wearing the shoes since the 1940s. 'We bought them because they were comfortable and the price was right.'

The brand struggled in the 1980s after facing strong competition from newcomers like Nike and the company went into bankruptcy in 2001. Nike eventually purchased them in 2003. However, in spite of its ups and downs the shoe still has myriad fans. Some consumers are drawn by the nostalgia; others are inspired by pop culture figures that wear the shoes, like the Ramones and Snoop Dogg.[1]

To celebrate its centennial, Converse hosted a series of concerts described as a 'striking artistic showcase of true originals that define the essence of the Converse brand since 1908'. The company also played on consumers' memories of the 'good old days' with their 'Connectivity' advertising campaign launched in 2008. The advertising campaign presents past and present Converse icons brought together to pay homage to the Chuck Taylor All Star shoe – from the Sex Pistol's Sid Vicious, to Green Day's Billy Joe Armstrong. The aim of the advertising is to encourage consumers of all ages to reconnect with the past via the Converse shoes. This nostalgia advertising strategy relies heavily on consumers generating positive memories about their past experiences with the shoe. This demonstrates how understanding memory and how it impacts upon consumers is of great importance to marketers.

Schema

Our knowledge of an object generally consists of the set of facts that we know and associate with that object. These associations are grouped together in a meaningful way to form a **schema** about that object. For instance, if asked about your knowledge regarding an orange, you might list the following attributes: round, sweet, fruit, breakfast food, vitamin C. All of these associations represent your schema for an orange. These associations could be physical attributes (round) or more abstract attributes (breakfast food).

Consumers have schemas for products (portable MP3 players, SUVs), brands (Nike, Microsoft) and stores (HMV, Gap). One type of schema that is important to companies is a product's **brand image**; this is a subset of associations that are related to a specific brand. Companies monitor their product's brand image very closely; they try to create the brand image that they believe would be best for the company's profitability through their advertising and other marketing efforts.

Running glossary

brand image
a subset of associations that are related to a specific brand

schema
associations with an object grouped together in a meaningful way

script
knowledge of a sequence of expected events in a given situation

script disruption
use of prior knowledge to grab consumers' attention by interrupting the script

script facilitation
use of prior knowledge to facilitate learning about new products or brands

Knowledge is of two kinds. We know a subject ourselves, or we know where we can find information on it.
Samuel Johnson

Marketers make use of schemas

Knowledge is usually represented by schemas that are made up of multiple associations with products, brands, stores and events. One type of schema is a **script**, which is our knowledge of a sequence of expected events in a given situation. For example, if you go to a restaurant you expect to follow a specific script – get a table; view the wine list; order drinks; view the menu; order appetizers; order the main course; order dessert; eat; pay for the meal. Marketers are aware that consumers store some knowledge in the form of scripts and use this information to help sell their products. Using consumer expectations to facilitate learning about new products or brands is called **script facilitation**. Alternatively, to grab consumers' attention, they can subvert expectations by interrupting the script; this is called **script disruption**. One company that made effective use of this technique is DirecTV. In an advertising campaign created by Deutsch Inc. of New York City, several movie clips are presented from popular older movies such as *Twister* and *Ferris Bueller's Day Off*. The consumers have very clear expectations of what they expect these familiar characters to say, but instead of the lines that they remember from the movie, the character subverts expectations by promoting DirecTV. These commercials performed as planned; they grabbed the consumer's attention and were favourably received by the target market.

It does not matter whether you are a small broker or part of a large financial institution. You still have to establish an identity that is unique from your competition. That identity is your brand image.

Jeffrey Nelson

< What is knowledge?
How is knowledge organised?
> How memory works

Consumers need to store a plethora of associations in the form of schemas and scripts in their memories and need a systematic method to organise this information. Consumer knowledge is generally organised into groups of related objects called **taxonomic categories**. Products are assigned some sort of identity and then grouped with products that are perceived as being similar. These categories also tend to be ordered in a hierarchical manner, for example, most people would store all shoes under 'footwear' (this is the **superordinate** category). But within this category they may also store different types of shoes in subcategories, such as running shoes and formal shoes (these are the **subordinate** categories).

Categorisation is important for marketers because during this process consumers make assumptions about a product's characteristics, competition and availability. In other words, in order to categorise a product a consumer has to decide what function it will perform, which other products might perform the same function, and finally where they might expect to buy the product (they might go to a showroom to buy a car but would be more comfortable buying music online).

Prototypes

Some items within a category are viewed as better representing the category than others; the original Coca-Cola and Pepsi soft drinks are better exemplars of the carbonated soda category than Diet Cherry Coke drinks. This process is known as **graded structure**. Within any category, consumers will rank products based on how well they perceive them to be representative of the category. In this context, the product that is perceived as best representing the category is known as the **prototype**. This is an advantageous position for any brand to be in since other brands will be compared to your product. Additionally, when consumers think of a particular category the prototype will tend to come to mind more quickly than other category members. For instance, Coca-Cola is considered to be the prototype for carbonated soft drinks across the world. This gives the Coca-Cola Company an advantage in marketing their product since it will be foremost in the minds of most consumers.

A better workout deserves better water! Propel Fitness Water and new Propel Calcium are sure to refresh your active body. They're both vitamin-enhanced and fitness focused with 10 calories so bodies in motion can stay in motion.

PepsiCo (Makers of Propel)

Nike is considered a prototype in the running-shoe market since it is thought of most frequently. Additionally, the brand has associations common with most running shoes, such as comfort, durability and performance. A prototype usually has an advantage over other brands since consumers would generally consider the prototype as one of the first choices when purchasing a product. However, other brands could still use consumers' knowledge of the prototype to their advantage. One possible strategy is to market your brand as being similar to the prototype brand. When this occurs, a large portion of the market opens up to the competing brand. In addition, consumers would consider purchasing this brand since the prototype to which it would be closely aligned is well-known and well-regarded by consumers.

When Gatorade introduced Propel Fitness Water in 2000, consumers had a difficult time categorising this new product. In order to make sense of this new entry into the marketplace, consumers either had to categorise it as a 'sports drink' or as 'water'.[2] Some established a new category, as Gatorade hoped they would: a 'sports or enhanced water'. Propel became very successful, partly due to its association with Gatorade, and sales topped $100 million in 2002. This success led to the introduction of line extensions in 2006, such as Propel Calcium (a low calorie drink) and Propel powder packets.

Running glossary

graded structure
a ranking of products based on how well they are representative of the category

prototype
a product that best represents a product category

subordinate
category below superordinate within taxonomic structure

superordinate
major category within basic level of taxonomic structure

taxonomic categories
knowledge that is organised into groups of similar objects

How memory works

The information that consumers store in their memories has a tremendous impact on their subsequent behaviour. Studies have shown that brands that can be easily recalled are more likely to be placed in the set of brands that a consumer considers for purchase.[3] Brands that are easily remembered are also better liked than other brands.[4] Consumers are continually acquiring, storing and retrieving information and marketers place great importance on how often consumers remember their brands.

Memory models

Recent models of memory view the human memory process as being very similar to the information-storing processes used by computers. Data is first collected externally and then processed in the RAM (Random access-memory) the information is then transferred to the ROM (read-only memory) and integrated with existing files for permanent storage. Finally, this information can be accessed and retrieved from the ROM when required.

As the diagram opposite illustrates, the human memory is very similar, with consumers first being exposed to external information in the form of different sensory outputs (visual, auditory and so on). This information is then encoded and transferred to sensory memory for a brief period, before moving to short-term memory – this is the brain's RAM. Then, if this information is further processed, it can be transferred to long-term memory (the equivalent of a computer's ROM) to be stored permanently and integrated with prior knowledge. There it will remain until needed; at which time it is retrieved from memory and placed into short-term memory for use.

The memory process

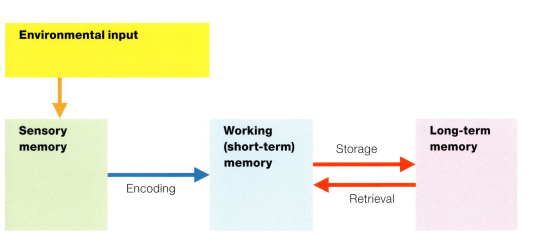

Environmental input

Sensory memory

Encoding

Working (short-term) memory

Storage

Retrieval

Long-term memory

The memory process
The memory process begins when an individual is exposed to external stimuli. This information is immediately encoded to sensory memory, before being transferred to short-term memory for up to 20 seconds. If further processing is required after this period the information is transferred to long-term memory. Finally, the individual can retrieve the information at a later date once prompted with the right cues; they might be faced with a purchase decision, for instance.[5]

Sensory memory

We are all exposed to numerous stimuli every day. It would be impossible to place all of the resulting information in our memories; our sensory memory therefore acts as a buffer between all of those external stimuli in the environment and our memory. We store information here on a very short-term basis (less than three seconds). For example, imagine you are driving and whiz by a billboard; you may see it quickly and be briefly aware that the billboard was advertising a Volvo car but may shortly afterwards have completely forgotten its existence.

We store many different types of sensory information, but the two major forms are **iconic** (memory for images) and **echoic** (memory for sounds). Information in sensory memory is stored for a few seconds. We move this information to working memory only if we are motivated to do so; for example, if we catch a glimpse of that ad for a Volvo automobile, we might pay additional attention to it and process it further if we were in the market for a new car.

Running glossary

discursive
relating to discourse or modes of discourse

echoic
sensory memory for sound

iconic
sensory memory for images

Short-term memory is electrical; long-term memory is chemical. We can only do three things to increase the transfer of our messages from electrical memory to chemical memory: increase the relevancy of the message, increase the frequency of its repetition, or both. Branding is accomplished only when you have a relevant message that is repeated with enough frequency to become stored in chemical memory.

Bryan and Jeff Eisenberg

Short-term memory

This space provides temporary storage for information currently in use (similar to the computer's RAM). Short-term memory has several attributes. It is very limited and can hold approximately seven bits of information, that is, we can generally only remember seven items at a time. It is of moderate duration; you cannot maintain information in short-term memory for more than 20 seconds. Attention is needed to move information into and out of short-term memory. In order for information to be retained in short-term memory, it must be rehearsed. Think of a new friend telling you their telephone number; if you have to remember that number for a short time before finding a pen and paper (or your own phone) you will have to repeat it a few times in order not to forget it immediately. By repeating the number to yourself, you will be able to maintain the information in short-term memory. If you are prevented from rehearsal, the information will simply decay from your short-term memory.

Discursive and imagery processing

We store information in short-term memory in two forms – as words (**discursive** processing) and as images (imagery processing). In the case of discursive processing, we would store an object as a basic label, e.g., beach. However, when we use imagery processing, we store the object visually as an approximation of the reality. Therefore, what we store in memory bears a closer resemblance to the actual object. In the case of the beach, we would store an image of the sand, water and waves.

Marketers have made use of consumers' ability to engage in imagery processing. Imagery facilitates the recall of past experiences. Vivid images allow us to relive events that we have experienced. For instance, seeing a photograph of an event that you attended is more likely to generate vivid memories, compared to seeing a sentence describing the event. So if a marketer for a holiday company wants to remind us how much fun it is to visit new places, a photograph of an exotic beach will usually be far more effective than a detailed description. A picture truly does 'speak a thousand words'.

〈 How is knowledge organised?
How memory works
〉 Case study: Nostalgia marketing – MINI

Long-term memory

This is a fairly permanent store of memory and is where consumers retain a lot of the knowledge that they acquire in their daily lives. Long-term memory has unlimited capacity. For information to be transferred from short-term to long-term memory, it must be processed more deeply and then associated with information that already exists in prior knowledge. The more deeply consumers process a particular piece of information, the more likely it is to be associated with existing information in memory; this information will then remain more accessible.

The importance of autobiographical memory

Long-term memory has been partitioned in two different ways. A lot of what we have stored in memory represents knowledge about experiences that we have had. This is known as **autobiographical/episodic memory**. These memories tap into the emotions that we felt during the original experiences and tend to be very powerful. Think about a very happy event in your life, such as success in an exam. Try to recall your experiences when you first heard the news. Depending on how recently the event occurred, the emotions and sensations that were attached to the event will also be part of the memory.

The other type of long-term memory is **semantic memory**. This is general or generic information about how things work in the world. For example, we have memory for an object called a car. We remember the car has tyres, seats and a steering wheel. We also know that if we get inside and turn the key, then the car should start and (assuming we know how) we would be able to drive it. This knowledge is separate from the memory for specific episodes in our life.

Marketers can use information stored in long-term memory to influence how consumers evaluate their products. As we mentioned earlier, consumers associate certain emotions with events in their life. Advertising that stimulates nostalgia can affect a consumer's evaluation of products that they associate with fondly remembered events. Coca-Cola does this very effectively in its 'Holidays are coming' annual campaign – stirring up memories of childhood excitement, Santa Claus and family gatherings.

Organisation of long-term memory

Information in long-term memory is organised according to meaningful relationships. This is called an associative network. For example, all information about cars could be stored closely together and connected via commonalities among the different bits of information. All SUVs might be connected and organised under that label. However, the Mercedes Benz SUV would also be connected to all other Mercedes Benz automobiles. Objects that have the most associations would be better remembered than items with fewer associations. The school you attended might have numerous associations, such as the different friends, teachers and new experiences you encountered there. Thus, you are more likely to remember your time at school than a less eventful period of your life.

Running glossary

autobiographical/episodic memory
long-term memory about experiences that we have had

semantic memory
general or generic information about how things work in the world

Memory is the greatest of artists, and effaces from your mind what is unnecessary.
Maurice Baring

Changing perceptions

In May 2003, the Volvo Car Corporation launched the S60R and the V70R. Volvo traditionally focuses on its safety image, but the launch of these new, sportier models marked a clear shift in direction as they touted the V70R as 'the fastest production wagon in North America' and boasted that 'the S60R can hit 60 mph in 5.4 seconds'.

Jay Hamill, marketing manager for Volvo Cars North America stated, 'Evolving is necessary. It's not easy to do, and safety is not going away. The role of the "R" is a halo – to provide an underlying image of total performance. But it will be a limited edition, for focus and exclusivity'.

Mr Hamill recognised that it would be difficult for consumers to view any Volvo as a sporty car given their existing knowledge of Volvo automobiles, especially since Volvo had a long-standing positioning as a safe family car. Volvo's dilemma highlights the impact of consumer knowledge on marketers. Consumers have different associations that they link to different products – in Volvo's case, 'safety' and 'family-friendliness'. These associations and other information make up the consumer's knowledge base. Consumers use this knowledge to interpret new information about cars in general, and Volvo cars in particular.[6]

As you search for memories of a particular event, your brain state progressively comes to resemble the state it was in when you initially experienced the event. It is all part of the brain's ability to cross-reference memories, pulling together separate pieces of information from an elaborate network of stored representations to recreate an event.

Sean Polyn

How is information retrieved from memory?

When a consumer is cued (or prompted) to retrieve information from memory, they start from the primary label under which all of the information for that subject is stored. They then move from that category label to other subcategories until they get to the memory that they need. When the first label is activated, in order to get to the concept that they are looking for in memory, this activation is 'spread' from one concept to another fairly automatically. This theory of spreading activation is illustrated in the 'Memory retrieval' figure on pp. 122–123.

To put this into context let's assume that a hunter is on the market for a certain type of dog. He may be cued by a print advert displaying new gear required for the upcoming hunting season. In this instance the label 'hunting dogs' may be activated as his current dogs may be getting too old to hunt. This activation in memory then spreads to his memory for sporting dogs. Since he is hunting small game, he may then recall the information he has in memory about retrievers. Thus from the initial cue, a process of recall is activated, spreading from label to label. This spread is facilitated by associations that lead the hunter through his existing memories. This happens until the desired information is retrieved – which breed of dog he should buy.

< How is knowledge organised?
How memory works
> Case study: Nostalgia marketing – MINI

✕

Memory retrieval: An associative network for dogs

When thinking about the need for a new dog for the hunting season, a hunter would likely begin with the broad category of 'dogs'. This activation in memory then spreads to his memory for 'hunting dogs'. Since he is hunting small game, he may then recall the information he has in memory about 'sporting dogs'. Thus from the initial cue, a process of recall is activated, spreading from label to label. This spread is facilitated by associations that lead the hunter through his existing memories. This happens until the desired information is retrieved – which breed of dog he should buy.

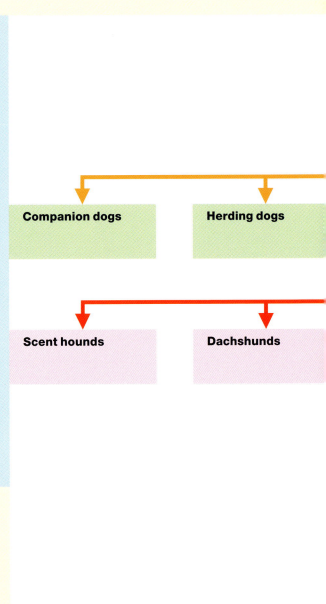

Companion dogs

Herding dogs

Scent hounds

Dachshunds

Retrievers

Setters

Memory retrieval: An associative network for dogs

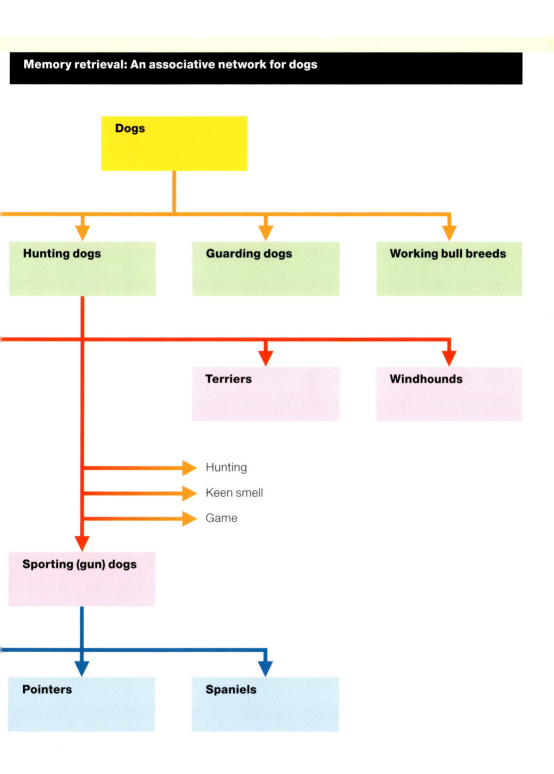

Background

In the 1950s the world was facing an oil shortage, when supplies were cut off due to the Suez Canal crisis. This threatened to put a damper on the British automobile industry, which was finally growing again after the Second World War. Given the possibility of restricted fuel supplies, the head of the British Motor Corporation (BMC), Sir Leonard Lord, challenged one of his designers, Alec Issigonis, to design an affordable, fuel-efficient car that could carry four adults. The result of Issigonis' design was the launch of two cars from BMC in 1959: the Austin Se7en and the Morris Mini-Minor. These 'MINIs' had a very compact design and the wheels were only ten inches in diameter to reduce the amount of intrusion into the interior passenger cabin space. In addition, the engine and transmission were mounted in a manner to maximise cabin room. The design allowed 80% of the MINI's total length to be dedicated to passenger cabin space. Thus, Sir Lord's dream was realised – a small, fuel-efficient car that could seat four adults. Primary competition for the MINI was the Volkswagen Beetle 1200, Renault Dauphine and Fiat 600. However, these cars were all rear engine with rear-wheel drive, whereas the MINI was front-wheel drive.

A partnership with John Cooper of the Cooper Car Company, which was known for its race cars, led to the development of the MINI Cooper. This was a high performance car with a larger engine and greater horse power. Rally-prepared MINI Coopers collected outright wins in the prestigious Monte Carlo Rally from 1964–1967. A number of wins in other competitions solidified the reputation of the MINI Cooper as a performance car.

The MINI became popular in many parts of the world and was manufactured in multiple countries under license to the British parent company, including Australia, Italy, Spain, Belgium, South Africa, Chile and Venezuela. In 1994, the company, now known as Rover, was sold to BMW. In 2000, BMW sold Land Rover to Ford and retained MINI. The remainder of the company became independent under the name MG Rover Group. In this environment of ownership upheaval, production of the MINI continued until 2000 when the last original MINI was produced.[7]

Fun MINI advertising

This advert for the new MINI uses a Transformer-style robot to appeal to the younger first-time buyers who might be less familiar with the original cars. At the same time, it emphasises fuel economy – a key selling point of the old MINI that will be very familiar to repeat customers.

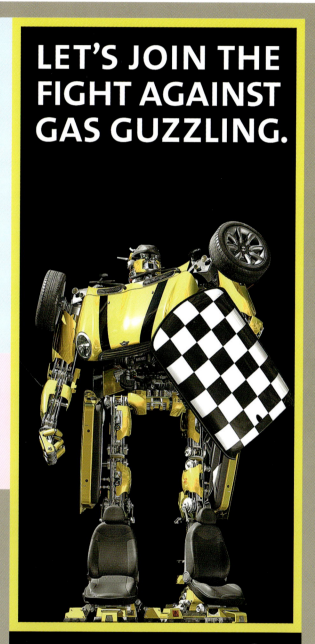

‹ How memory works
Case study / Nostalgia marketing – MINI
› Questions and exercises

MINIs – new and old

Many people complained that the new MINI was not a 'real' MINI. They believed there were too many changes made to the original: however, there is a clear family resemblance between the original shown bottom left and the new design above.

© BMW AG

The new MINI

BMW continued to develop the MINI automobile. However, the company scrapped the work Rover had done and pursued a new design for a replacement MINI. Their intent was to redesign the MINI along the lines on which the original might have evolved if it had kept up with changes in the automotive world. They wanted to design a modern car that was still instantly recognisable as a MINI. These new cars would all be known as MINI Coopers.

The MINI Cooper first became available in Europe during 2001. This was followed by the MINI Cooper S a few months later. The first MINIs were available for sale in the US in April 2002.

Using nostalgia

Marketing the new MINI presented an interesting challenge. Much like the original model, the new MINI was marketed as a fuel-efficient car, with a surprising amount of interior space. BMW hoped its marketing efforts would help generate feelings of nostalgia. The aim was to tap into the positive memories of older MINI enthusiasts who were familiar with the fuel economy and surprising roominess of the original MINI and the racing success of the MINI Cooper. The company hoped that this nostalgia would lead to customers wanting to try and then purchase the new MINI.

In addition, BMW also targeted young, affluent drivers between 20–34 years old. The updated design and modern conveniences of the redesigned MINI were aimed at these new drivers. The company believed that the updated design could help revive the somewhat dormant MINI brand while also providing it with new brand meaning and developing a new brand story for first-time buyers.

Most industry analysts thought the world's desire for one of the best-known microcars would have long declined. Yet the original, popular as it was during its peak sales period, was not a modern design even though it saw many updates and improvements over its lifetime. In order to keep up with the times, BMW had to add some innovative new features to make the MINI contemporary. The marketing strategy proved a great success. Sales of the new MINI rose from its launch and peaked in 2005 at 200,000 units, with projected sales dipping to 180,000 in 2006. The rising price of gas in 2008 led to a resurgence in demand for the new MINI and sales again rose. 'The world's leading premium small car', as BMW likes to call it, now accounts for more than 15% of the company's sales worldwide.

Other brands use of 'nostalgia marketing'

Other companies have also turned to nostalgia marketing in their attempts to revive their brands. For example, Michelin resurrected the 109-year-old Michelin man for a 2007 television campaign. In addition, after a five-year absence, Cadbury reintroduced its 'Flake girl', who featured in a long-running campaign that was voted Britain's favourite in television poll. Other car manufacturers have adopted similar strategies. For example, Volkswagen rolled out the new Beetle in 1998 and Fiat also began selling an updated version of its classic 500 in 2007. The brand equity created by these brands over the years is hard to throw away and so companies try to remake these old brands and brand images by presenting them in a contemporary way. Using classic brands also makes financial sense as it takes a great deal of advertising dollars to create a new brand image; by tapping into existing memories companies can save on advertising costs as ads to drum up initial awareness are therefore not necessary.

Gerry Moira, director of UK creativity at Euro RSCG likened reviving an old brand to 're-using bricks to build a new house'. The costs are substantially reduced and the result is still a very sturdy structure.

Question 1

What are some of the major advantages and disadvantages of nostalgia marketing?

Question 2

Are there some products or brands for which this strategy may not be successful? Why not?

Question 3

Develop a 'nostalgia marketing' campaign for an old brand that is declining or that no longer exists. To whom would you target the brand? How would you position the brand (how would you want consumers to perceive it)? How would you price it? Where would you sell it? What would the new product look like? Would it be updated in any way? How would you advertise it?

Discussion questions

1

Knowledge is generally comprised of associations with different objects. What are the different characteristics of these associations?

2

What are the two different ways in which a company can make use of schema in their marketing tactics? Provide your own examples of each.

3

When consumers encounter new objects they go through the process of categorisation. In what ways could categorisation be important to marketers?

4

Describe how the two main types of sensory memory differ from each other.

5

What are the characteristics of short-term memory? How could we use short-term memory to market more effectively to consumers?

6

Describe the spreading activation theory of memory retrieval.

Exercise 1

Visit your local grocery store. While walking through the aisle, make a note of where products are located on the shelves. Are there any brands that you would categorise as belonging to another product category, even though it is located in a specific location on the shelf? For instance, Propel Fitness Water might be located near Gatorade, but you might still categorise it as water and not a fitness drink. Note these examples and present them in class, along with your reasons for categorising them differently. Do you believe that this mistaken categorisation is beneficial or harmful to the manufacturer?

Exercise 2

Along with three of your classmates, select a food that at least one of you likes. Develop a schema for that food – include both positive and negative associations. As a company that markets that food product, how could you make use of some of the more salient positive associations in your marketing campaign? How would you counter any negative associations?

Exercise 3

Conduct a memory experiment. Provide a list of eight product attributes (for **one** product) to three different individuals. Interview each person separately. Let each individual read the list for 15 seconds. Take the list away then perform a distracter task – ask your friend to count backwards in threes from 100 (100, 97, 94, 91). Do this for 30 seconds. Then ask them to try to remember the list of attributes that you showed them. What are your results? What does this tell you about how consumer memory works?

Endnotes

1
Hosten, K. 'Legions of Converse Fans stay loyal to Chuck Taylor Sneakers' 21 March 2007, <www.theledger.com>

2
Day, S. 'Bottled Water is Still Pure, but is it Water anymore' *The New York Times,* 3 August 2002

3
Desai, K. K. and Hoyer, W. D. December 2000, 'Descriptive Characteristics of Memory-Based Consideration Sets: Influence of Usage Occasion on Frequency and Usage Location Familiarity'; *Journal of Consumer Research*

4
Menon, G. and Raghubir, P. May 2003, 'Ease-of-Retrieval as an Automatic Input in Judgments: A Mere-Accessibility Framework?' *Journal of Consumer Research* (pp. 230–243)

5
© 2001 Houghton Mifflin Company. All rights reserved

6
Rechtin, M. 'Volvo enters fast lane with impending launch of sporty R models' *Automotive News,* 22 April 2003

7
Frost, P. 'Classic Mini Cooper' *Businessweek,* 15 June 2007

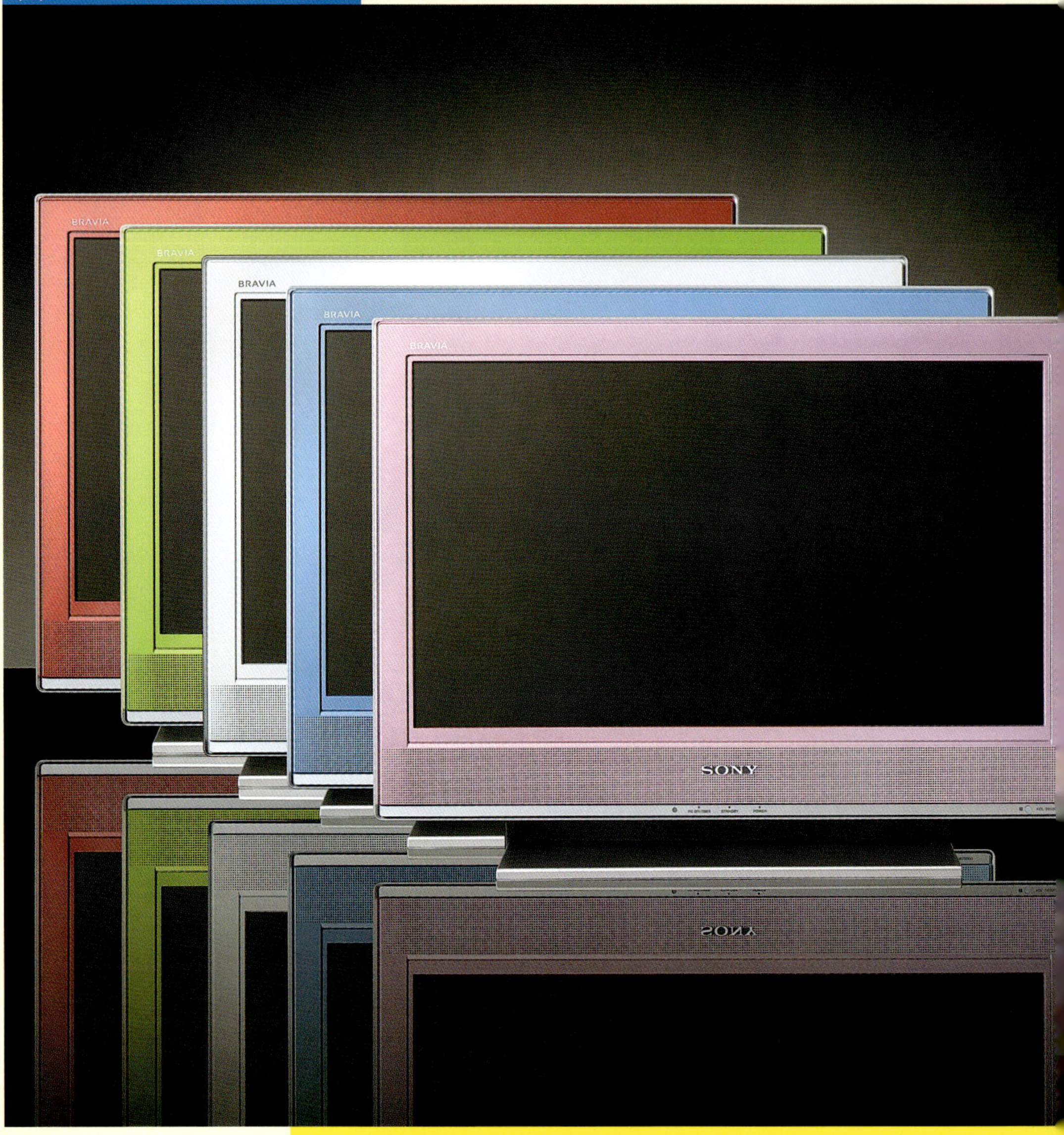
BRAVIA
BRAVIA
BRAVIA
BRAVIA
BRAVIA
SONY

✕

BRAVIA S Series LCD – Multi-colour group shot

When deciding on a big purchase like a new television most consumers begin with an internal search of their memory for any existing relevant information. If they don't have pre-existing knowledge, then they may search externally, using the Internet or consumer magazines.

© Sony Electronics

In November 2006 Wal-Mart, the largest American retailer, slashed prices on their 42-inch flat-panel televisions. Other large electronics retailers followed suit, until by the end of 2007 the average price fall on LCD television sets was 30%.[1] Lured by these lower prices and advertising that stressed the flat-screen televisions realistic picture and sharp colours, many consumers began their search for the perfect model at the right price. So, how did they make their choices?

Throughout this chapter we will examine this process of consumer decision making – from customers realising that they have a need to satisfy, then searching for information, evaluating the options and making the purchase. Finally, we examine the need for companies to respond to consumers after the purchase is made.

Consumers make decisions on a daily basis – from which mode of transportation to take to work to which type of meal to consume for lunch or dinner. Why would this process be important to marketers?

Marketers need to know why consumers choose one product over another. Why purchase a BMW instead of a Mercedes? Why Nike instead of Adidas? Understanding consumers' preferences and how they make decisions enables marketers to influence the choice process and determine how best to persuade consumers to examine their brand and place it in the group of items being considered for purchase.

Essential assumptions

The theory of decision making rests on some basic assumptions. The most important is that there is more than one alternative available. If there is no competition, then the decision for the consumer would not be which brand to purchase, but whether or not to buy the product at all. In the case of some products with limited or no alternatives, such as gas and electricity provided by municipalities, then the decision to purchase is already made for the consumer, lessening the need for marketing. Additionally, we assume that the consumer must choose from the multiple brands available to them. Finally, we assume that the consumer will choose the best possible option that suits their needs.

Traditional television broadcast advertising strives to raise consumer awareness of a product or service, in the hope that a consumer will remember that product or brand when making a purchasing decision.
David Mandelbrot

The internal process

Consumer decision making is one of the most important internal processes studied by marketers. First, a consumer will realise that they have a problem (they are exposed to a product that could simplify their life). Next they search for information that would help them in their decision making, before making a judgment about the product to be purchased – would they be satisfied with this item? The consumer will then make a choice or decision regarding the final purchase – to buy or not to buy? If they do make a purchase, some individuals may experience post-purchase regret – that uneasy feeling in your stomach and the voice in your head that whispers, 'Did I make the right choice?'

This dissonance is only one of several different feelings that we experience post-purchase. As we shall see, successful marketers know how to effectively manage this process from beginning to end, including dealing with dissatisfied customers after purchase.

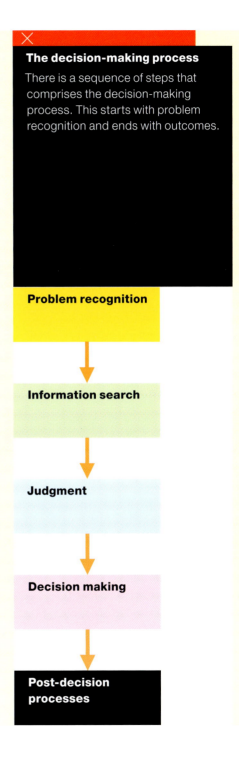

The decision-making process

There is a sequence of steps that comprises the decision-making process. This starts with problem recognition and ends with outcomes.

Problem recognition

Information search

Judgment

Decision making

Post-decision processes

Seeing a need

The first step in the decision-making process is recognising that a need exists. When a consumer decides to make a purchase it is in response to a problem – 'I need a new computer' or 'I am hungry and would like some food'. Problem recognition occurs whenever the consumer sees a significant difference between their actual state of affairs and some desired or ideal state.

The 'ideal state' is the way the consumer would like to be, 'I would like a new 42-inch flat-screen television', and the actual state is where they are now, 'I am still viewing television on a 13-inch black-and-white television'. Problem recognition occurs when consumers notice the discrepancy between the two states, 'my television is a very old model'. The 'problem recognition' figure shown opposite illustrates the two ways in which this process occurs.

Problem recognition

There are two distinct types of problem recognition: the first is need recognition, which occurs when there is a decrease in the actual state (for example, 'I'm running out of milk; I should go to the grocery store to buy some'). The second type is opportunity recognition, which occurs when there is an increase in the ideal state (for example, 'I saw a flat-screen HDTV at my friend's house. The image is much better than the television that I have at home. I am going to buy one').

Once you make a decision, the universe conspires to make it happen.
Ralph Waldo Emerson

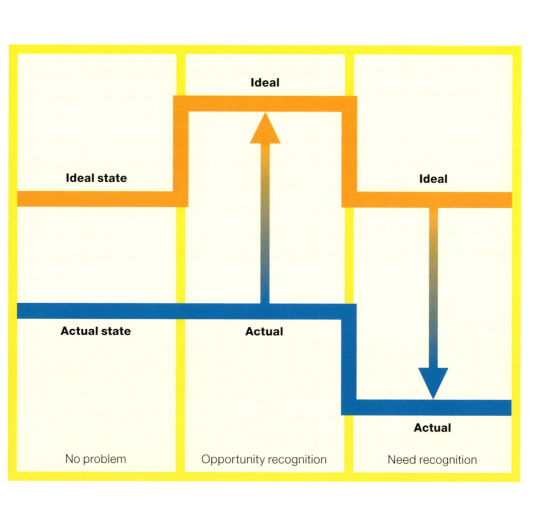

Ideal

Ideal state

Ideal

Actual state

Actual

Actual

No problem

Opportunity recognition

Need recognition

Problem recognition

Motivating problem recognition

Many marketers attempt to motivate consumers to initiate the decision-making process by identifying potential problems through advertising. They do this by either creating a new ideal state or by creating dissatisfaction with the actual state. By stimulating problem recognition, companies encourage consumers to pursue a means of solving their new 'problem'.

To put this into context, companies that sell exercise equipment and dietary supplements sometimes use 'before and after' imagery to create a new ideal state. Even if a consumer is in reasonably good shape this type of advertising can still motivate them to want to look better than they do at the moment and so they need to try and resolve a newly found 'problem'. This problem is caused by a shift in the consumer's ideal state – 'I could look like that'. Once a consumer accepts that they have a new problem then the marketer can position their brand as the best way to solve that problem.

Using generic problem recognition

Problem recognition may be classified in two ways. Consumers engage in **generic** or **selective problem recognition**. Generic problem recognition is broadly defined, 'I want orange juice', whereas secondary problem recognition is more narrowly defined, 'I want Tropicana orange juice'.

Companies or groups that want to stimulate growth in a specific product category make extensive use of advertising that promotes generic problem recognition and does not encourage purchase of a specific brand, as can be seen in the Got Milk? example described opposite.

Running glossary

generic problem recognition
broadly defined

selective problem recognition
narrowly defined

A real decision is measured by the fact that you've taken a new action. If there's no action, you haven't truly decided.
Anthony Robbins

Got Milk?

Faced with declining milk sales in the state of California, the California Milk Processor Board CMPB launched the now famous Got Milk? campaign in October 1993 to help increase milk consumption. This campaign went national throughout the US and helped resuscitate milk sales after a 20-year slump. After years of advertising claiming that milk was 'good for you', the new campaign turned the ad world upside down by dramatising the dire consequences of eating snacks and other foods and not drinking milk.

The first spot to run in 2003 was titled 'Aaron Burr'. The spot opens on an American history buff stuffing a huge peanut butter sandwich into his mouth and listening to a classical music radio channel. The DJ announces a $10,000 trivia question, 'Who shot Alexander Hamilton?' Alexander Hamilton, the founder of the first political party in the United States, the Federalist Party, was killed in a duel by Aaron Burr.

The camera pans an apartment of the history buff who obviously knows the answer. His apartment is filled with memorabilia from the famous duel, including a portrait of Burr and the actual bullet preserved in a glass curio. Mouth crammed and unable to respond, the pitiful history buff reaches for the milk only to find it empty. Desperate, he can only mutter 'Aaaawon Buuuuhh'. The spot ends with the now familiar 'got milk?'

The Got Milk? campaign had over 90% awareness nationally and the tag line has been licensed to dairy boards around the country since 1995. This campaign evolved into the famous milk moustache campaign. Here celebrities are depicted as milk drinkers; the evidence – a thin milk moustache. The Got Milk? campaign was aimed at creating generic problem recognition. Sales of all brands of milk increased after the campaign started.[2]

Information search

After a consumer recognises that they have a problem, they then have to find information to help them resolve it. The first step in this search process is **internal search** – searching in the consumer's own memory. This is followed by a search through external sources (information collected through advertising and other external media).

In addition to *where* consumers search for information, it is also important to consider *when* they search. Most consumers search for information pre-purchase to help ensure that they make an optimal purchase to satisfy their needs. Alternatively, an information search can also be ongoing. This often occurs if the consumer is a collector of a certain type of product, such as vintage automobiles. In this case, they would continually check data sources to see whether or not the cars are available for sale.

External search for information

Marketers often assume that consumers collect as much information as possible in order to find the product or service that best satisfies their needs. However, this is not always the case. Consumers weigh the cost of getting additional information (time and effort) against the benefit the information could provide, such as a cheaper or more suitable product. If their most pressing need is to have the product quickly then they may be willing to forego any research into price and quality and simply purchase the most easily available option.

However, in recent times it has become easier to gather information about products and so consumers are able to spend less time collecting information. For example, if a consumer is interested in buying a new car, in addition to searching through memory, they can also locate information via print, television and billboard advertising. Additionally, consumers visit company websites to collect additional information such as technical specifications. They can also visit websites that provide reviews such as <www.consumerreports.org>.

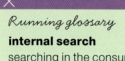

Running glossary

internal search
searching in the consumer's own memory

Does prior knowledge impact on information search?

Who would you expect to undertake the most research before purchasing a product? Would it be an expert, a novice or someone in the middle who has moderate knowledge? Researchers investigating this question found some surprising results.[3] When presented with an array of information about automobiles, consumers who were making an automobile purchase had different search patterns depending on their existing knowledge of cars. Consumers with moderate knowledge actually searched for and recalled the most information. Both novices and experts searched less and eventually recalled less information from their search.

The researchers believed that consumers with no knowledge focused on known and easily comparable attributes (brand, price, others' opinions and so on), which may not have always led to optimal decisions, but resulted in a quick search. On the other hand, experts paid attention only to the most relevant information (performance, fuel economy and so on) and processed the information quickly as well. A point to ponder: why do you think individuals with moderate knowledge performed the most effective information search?

An expert is someone who has succeeded in making decisions and judgments simpler through knowing what to pay attention to and what to ignore.

Edward de Bono

The next stage in the consumer's decision-making process is their judgment about the product to be purchased – 'will this product do what I want it to do?' And finally making a choice or decision regarding the final purchase – 'should I buy it or not?'

For high-risk purchases, consumers invest a lot of effort into making judgments and decisions. These high-effort situations usually occur when there is some risk involved – such as health (selecting a doctor, for example), financial (buying a house), or social (selecting a partner).

To help with this process, consumers sometimes use an anchoring strategy. They base their initial evaluation on a known value and then adjust their evaluations based on additional information when it becomes available – suggestions from friends, reviews, or even experience through trial.[4] The initial evaluation could be influenced by the reputation of the brand – this is the consumer's initial 'anchor'. The evaluation can then be reassessed once the product is seen and examined more closely. At this point the consumer would either adjust their evaluation upward or downward depending on the actual quality of the item.

Country-of-origin effects

One method of anchoring is country of origin. For example, clothing that is made in Italy is synonymous with high quality. When a consumer sees that clothing is made in Italy, they immediately infer that the product is well made. However, country-of-origin effects can also be negative. Many Western consumers perceive products manufactured in China as being cheaply made and with limited durability. Consumers anchor their initial evaluation on the country where the product is made using this kind of preconception and subsequently adjust their judgment upward or downward after they have used the product, based on actual performance. However, the initial evaluation often has the greatest impact on the final judgment, since consumers can be slow to adjust their evaluations a great deal.[5]

Moving from problem recognition to final decision

When a consumer realises that they have a problem, they must determine which products or services will best help solve the problem; for example, which make and model of automobile should they buy now that they have moved 90 minutes from their job?

As illustrated on pp. 144–145, the consumer conducts an internal search and retrieves several different cars from memory. This is known as the **retrieved set**. After internal search, the consumer then proceeds through external search. Together with the initial subset of brands found in memory, these new items are combined to form the **evoked set**. Then all of the brands that the consumer deems acceptable are placed in the **consideration set** – those brands that they would consider for purchase. Once the brands in the consideration set have been evaluated, the consumer decides to purchase the brand which best satisfies their needs.

Good judgment comes from experience. Experience comes from bad judgment.
Jim Horning

Running glossary

consideration set
all brands that the consumer deems acceptable for purchase

evoked set
external search combined with retrieved set

retrieved set
internal search and retrieval of several memories

 ⟨ Consumer decision making
Judgment and decision making
 ⟩ What influences consumers' decisions?

Evaluation: Narrowing the alternatives

When a consumer recognises that they have a problem that requires a purchase to resolve it, they go through three distinct phases. Firstly, an internal search for valuable information already stored in their memory (retrieved set), then an external search which, combined with the information already found in their memory, forms the evoked set. Finally, the most relevant brands are placed in the consideration set before the final decision is made.

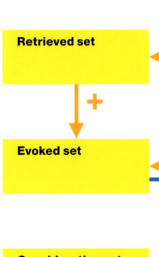

Retrieved set

Evoked set

Consideration set

Chosen brand

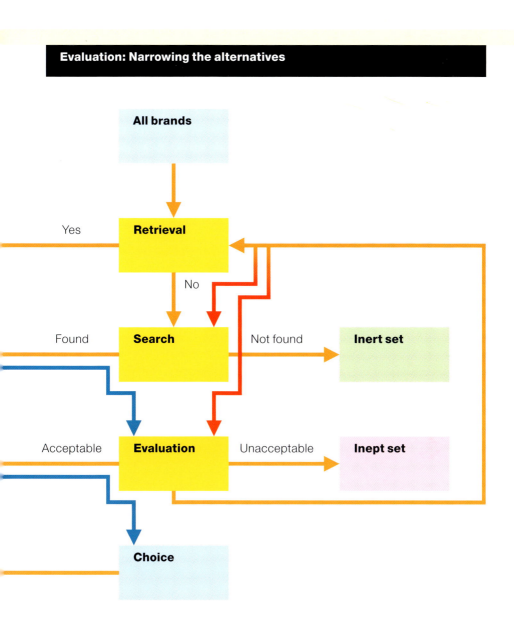

Evaluation: Narrowing the alternatives

< Judgment and decision making
What influences consumers' decisions?
> Post-decision processes

How do people choose the products and brands that they finally decide to use? Over the last 30 years experimental psychologists have documented different factors that can impact on consumer decision making; two of the biggest are context effects and task effects.

The context-effects concept describes how different elements of the environment can impact on how consumers perceive a stimulus. This is known as a 'top-down' theory and illustrates how consumers include sensory information – what they see, hear, smell and so on – in their cognitive processes when trying to understand what a stimulus means. For instance, sometimes consumer decision making can be altered simply by changing the objects that surround the product the consumer is considering for purchase.

*The term 'frame dependence'
means that the way people behave
depends on the way that their
decision problems are 'framed'.*
Hersh Shefrin

Framing

Framing is a decision-making process in which people reach conclusions based on the 'framework' within which a certain situation is presented. People who believe that all choices are rational assume that no matter how a problem is described, as long as the salient facts remain the same then the same choices should be made. However, contrary to this assertion, there is evidence that variations in how options are presented or 'framed' can result in very different choices being made.[6]

One such framing effect theory has been termed '**loss aversion**'. Psychologists believe that losses loom larger than corresponding gains. Two researchers from Stanford University, Amos Tversky and Daniel Kahneman, first described the idea of loss aversion as the tendency for people to strongly prefer avoiding losses than acquiring gains. The central assumption of the theory is that losses and disadvantages have greater impact on preferences than gains and advantages. Their studies suggest that losses can be twice as psychologically powerful as gains.[7] It is therefore beneficial for marketers to 'frame' their product's attributes as gains instead of losses. For instance, a yoghurt manufacturer selling a product that contains 5% fat might advertise it as 95% fat-free.

Task effects

Task effects refer to the complexity of the purchasing decision – if there are a lot of alternatives and required attributes, for example, this might make a purchasing decision more difficult. Additionally, if consumers are under a time constraint the task can become even more complex. Therefore, although it is commonly assumed that consumers use all of the information available to them to choose the most suitable product, this is not necessarily always the case. In general, consumers do indeed engage in a lot of thought and research for high-effort decisions. However, for complex, low-effort decisions consumers tend to use **heuristics** – which are simplified decision rules that can be used as shortcuts to make decisions, such as price and brand name.[8] There are two major heuristics used by consumers: representativeness and availability.

Representativeness

When the decision is a low-effort one, consumers sometimes compare the current option to the prototype or category exemplar, i.e. the product that best represents the category. For example, there have been many instances of competing soft drinks labelling and packaging their products to look very similar to Coca-Cola. When consumers make the comparison, products that are close to the prototype are often evaluated more favourably.

Availability

For low-effort decisions, consumer decisions are also impacted by the ease with which instances of an event can be brought to mind. If a consumer has received several recommendations for a new brand of soda via word-of-mouth communication, then that brand would be more likely to come to mind and it would be evaluated favourably by the consumer when they want a drink. To take advantage of this strategy, marketers provide consumers with positive and vivid product-related experiences through advertising; this should enhance availability of the brand in the consumer's mind.

Running glossary

framing
a decision-making process in which people tend to reach conclusions based on the framework within which a situation was presented

heuristics
simplified decision rules that could be used as shortcuts to make decisions, such as price and brand name

loss aversion
the tendency for people to strongly prefer avoiding losses than acquiring gains

< Judgment and decision making
What influences consumers' decisions?
> Post-decision processes

Consumer's simplifying tactics

Consumers use a variety of strategies to try to simplify the decision process in low-effort situations. These include price strategies (buy the least expensive or the most expensive, depending on the quality required); normative strategies (go along with recommendations from friends); variety-seeking tactics (buy something different from the last time). Another simplifying strategy is habit. Consumers sometimes buy the product that they are accustomed to buying. One way of increasing this kind of brand loyalty is to offer repeat or frequent buyer programmes. Companies such as Starbucks have great success with these loyalty cards. Once the consumer has purchased a certain number of items they receive a free item or a discount on their purchase. Continuing use of these cards increases brand loyalty, especially for low-effort products.

Table 1

Weight

Price

Table 2

Weight

Price

Table 3

Weight

Price

Power

Number of attachments

Task effects: How decisions become more complex

Hoover	Royal
22 lbs	30 lbs
$230	$149

Hoover	Royal	Kenmore	Electrolux	Kirby
22 lbs	30 lbs	18 lbs	20 lbs	22 lbs
$230	$149	$250	$225	$199

Hoover	Royal	Kenmore	Electrolux	Kirby
22 lbs	30 lbs	18 lbs	20 lbs	22 lbs
$230	$149	$250	$225	$199
9 amps	11 amps	12 amps	12 amps	10 amps
4	4	7	5	5

✕

Task effects: How decisions become more complex
As can be seen in this example using vacuum cleaners, the decision-making process can become more complex by:
■ increasing the number of alternatives in the choice set (Table 2)
■ increasing the number of attributes in the choice set (Table 3).

Marketers are aware that after consumers have made their decision and have purchased a product, their job is not complete. Companies need to manage their post-decision interaction with buyers in order to maintain a long-term profitable relationship with them. This entails making sure that the consumer is satisfied with their purchase and any concerns or feelings of 'buyer's remorse' are dealt with effectively by the company.

American Customer Satisfaction Index

According to the American Customer Satisfaction Index, the level of dissatisfaction with many services has risen sharply over the past five years. These include hotels, airlines, Internet travel, broadcast television, and Internet search engines. Many businesses have not realised the importance of customer satisfaction to their long-term profitability and survival.

Satisfaction and dissatisfaction

Satisfied customers are often repeat purchasers and this leads to greater profitability. Additionally, repeat customers help to reduce costs. The cost of attracting a new customer is five times the cost of keeping an existing one. Thus, a business that maintains its loyal customer base, in addition to building its market with new customers, has the best chance for long-term survival.

Equally, dissatisfied customers can directly impact a company's bottom line through reduced sales. Dissatisfied customers stop purchasing; they can also complain and spread negative word of mouth. One reason why businesses should pay attention to their dissatisfied customers is that they may just be the tip of the proverbial iceberg. The average business does not hear from 96% of its unhappy customers. However, the average person who has had a major problem with a company tells around ten people. For most businesses, a quick response is the best solution – 95% of unhappy customers will continue to do business with a company if their complaint is resolved quickly.

So what are the mechanisms at work after consumers make a purchase? What theories could help marketers understand how customers evaluate their decisions after the purchase has been made? Two theories that shed some light on this process are **cognitive dissonance** theory and the theory of satisfaction.

Cognitive dissonance

The final stage for a consumer is the post-purchase evaluation of the decision they made. It is common for customers to experience concerns after making a purchase decision. This arises from a concept known as 'cognitive dissonance'.

Cognitive dissonance is caused by feelings of uncertainty as to whether or not one has made the right decision. This is most likely to occur when there are multiple attractive alternatives or when there is potential for risk in the consumption of the item. So how do consumers and businesses respond to cognitive dissonance? Consider a young man purchasing an engagement ring for his fiancée. In examining rings, he realises that there are thousands of different rings, with different style, cut and clarity. The dissonance is made worse by the price of the ring. This can only be relieved if his intended bride is pleased with his choice.

A consumer who is experiencing dissonance after his or her purchase may try to return the product or may seek positive information about it to justify the choice. If the buyer is unable to justify the purchase, they will be less likely to purchase that brand again. Since dissonance can lead to returns or no repeat purchase it is important for marketers to minimise any potential for dissonance in the consumer. Indeed, some marketers spend the majority of their advertising budget on advertising that reassures existing consumers that purchasing their product is the right choice. This is especially true of durable goods. Additionally, automobile manufacturers provide long-term warranties on their vehicles. This gives car buyers the reassurance that their vehicle would be covered in case anything happened to the vehicle. Some companies also provide free-phone services to give consumers advice if they experience any problems with the product post-purchase. This type of support sends a comforting message to consumers – the company cares about the customer and their purchase.

Running glossary

cognitive dissonance
the uncertainty as to whether one made the right decision

**Theory of satisfaction –
expectation disconfirmation model**

One theory that explains how customers are satisfied is the expectation disconfirmation model. This theory is based on the belief that individuals evaluate the outcomes of their purchase decisions after using the product or service based on their initial expectations. If the product met their needs and expectations, then they would be satisfied. If not, this would lead to dissatisfaction. Imagine taking a trip to a new restaurant that has received rave reviews in the local papers; this would lead you to expect a certain level of quality and taste when you visit. Therefore, if the meal and service are only average, then you might be dissatisfied. Alternatively, if your expectation of a certain restaurant is low (for example, in an airport you might expect the food to be flavourless and overpriced) then an 'average' experience with reasonable prices and fairly tasty food would leave you satisfied.

Thus, the basic assumption of the expectation disconfirmation model is that consumer satisfaction depends on pre-consumption expectations. If there is a discrepancy between our prior expectations, whether they are met or not, and our actual experience, then disconfirmation occurs.

In this model, the consumer's experience with the product is termed performance. Most performance evaluations are subjective, since they are the customer's evaluation of whether or not the expected outcome was achieved. As seen in the diagram opposite, if performance is better than expected then **positive disconfirmation** occurs and this results in satisfaction. Satisfaction also occurs in the case of simple confirmation – performance equals expectations. If performance is worse than expectations then **negative disconfirmation** occurs and this leads to dissatisfaction.

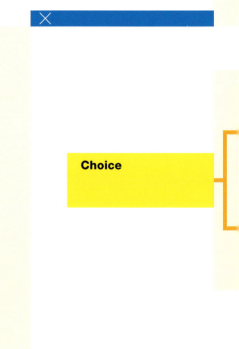

Choice

×

Running glossary

negative disconfirmation
performance is less than expected

positive disconfirmation
performance is better than expected

×

Expectation disconfirmation model
The expectation disconfirmation model can explain how consumers become satisfied or dissatisfied. If performance exceeds expectations (leading to positive disconfirmation), then the consumer would be satisfied. This is also true if performance is equal to expectations. If performance is less than expected (leading to negative disconfirmation) then the consumer will be dissatisfied.[9]

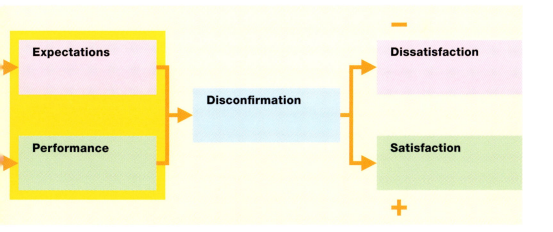

Expectation disconfirmation model

Background

JetBlue Airways was launched in February 2001 with its hub in New York City. In addition to discounted fares, JetBlue focused on customer service and this helped to grow their customer base. Their customer comforts included all-leather seats, and in-flight entertainment such as 36 channels of satellite television, 100 channels of XM Satellite Radio and pay-per-view movies. JetBlue was recognised for its superior customer service by J.D. Power Associates and *Aviation Week* magazine who conducted a survey of 10,000 discount airline customers in 2005 and 2006. JetBlue received the highest ratings of overall airline satisfaction. They ranked the highest using such factors as cost and fees; quality of flight crew, including courtesy and appearance; in-flight services; ease of check-in; and timeliness of boarding.

In addition to the J.D. Power and Associates distinction, the company consistently topped rankings for customer satisfaction, winning the University of Nebraska's national Airline Quality Rating study each year since 2003 and receiving five consecutive Readers' Choice Awards from *Condé Nast Traveler*. However, the airline's position as the model of customer service and operational efficiency was threatened after a memorable failure on Valentine's Day 2007.

The Valentine's Day debacle

Weather could spell serious problems for any airline's departure schedule and on 14 February 2007 weather forecasters predicted a winter ice storm which would eventually turn to rain. With that forecast in mind, JetBlue staff at John F. Kennedy Airport loaded flights and allowed them to taxi to the runway. However, the wintry conditions did not change as predicted. In addition, planes continued to land and, due to the poor weather, FAA regulations prevented flights from taking off. This led to only 17 of JetBlue's 156 scheduled departures leaving JFK. This in turn led to a ripple effect throughout the system, displacing crew and aircraft. In the following days JetBlue cancelled additional flights; these cancellations led to thousands of passengers being stranded. Finally, on 20 February, normal operations resumed.

In addition to JetBlue, other airlines also experienced major delays due to the bad weather. On that day, approximately 97% of all flights at JFK were either cancelled or delayed, with up to 80% of the flights being cancelled. However, JetBlue experienced the longest delays of all the major carriers. Before the airline's employees could round up buses to bring the passengers back to the terminal from the marooned jets, some travellers had been stuck on planes for as long as ten hours.[10]

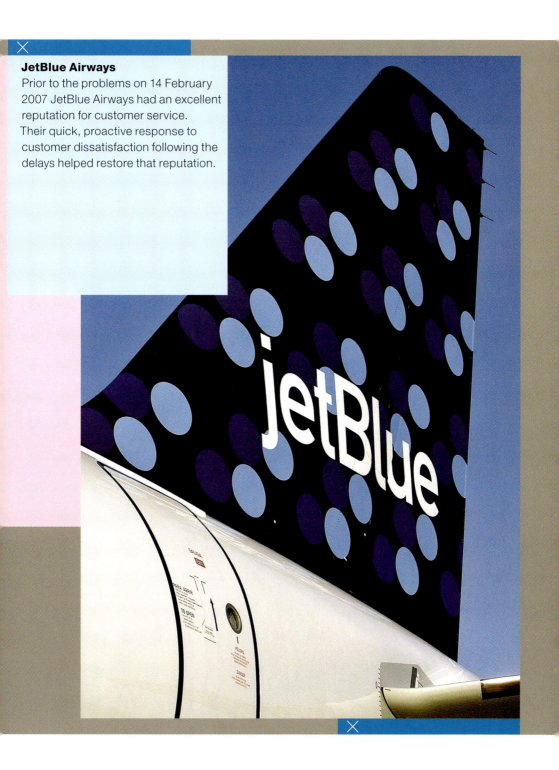

JetBlue Airways
Prior to the problems on 14 February 2007 JetBlue Airways had an excellent reputation for customer service. Their quick, proactive response to customer dissatisfaction following the delays helped restore that reputation.

‹ Post-decision processes
Case study / JetBlue Airway's Valentine's Day debacle
› Questions and exercises

JetBlue's response

JetBlue accepted responsibility for the problems and on 15 February, the company announced that passengers delayed on-board any aircraft for more than three hours would receive a full refund and a voucher for a free round-trip flight.

The airline also employed several approaches to reduce the backlog of passengers held up by the storm. They added flights to some destinations and booked passengers on other airlines. On 19 February, CEO David Neeleman posted a video apology to JetBlue customers on the company's website and on the video-sharing website YouTube. He also posted a written apology on the JetBlue site and sent emails directly to each passenger affected by the disruption. Neeleman even made a damage-control appearance on the *Late Show with David Letterman* where he promised that the airline was going to 'learn from the experience like nothing that's ever happened to us before'.

Immediately after the Valentine's Day events, JetBlue became an object of anger and scorn among travellers and politicians alike. Many passengers called for boycotts of JetBlue, in spite of its previous reputation for quality service. This single, major service failure had led to an erosion of the goodwill that the airline had built up with its passengers over the years. However, airline industry analysts believed that JetBlue's immediate response, and the policies implemented shortly thereafter were critical in remaking its tarnished image.

Question 1

What could JetBlue have done on 14 February in response to the customer dissatisfaction?

Question 2

Were the airline's efforts after the incident enough to regain their customers' trust? If not, what else could they have done in the days and months after the incident?

Question 3

How would you have shown your dissatisfaction on that day and in the month after?

Bill of Rights

On 21 February 2007 JetBlue issued a *Customer Bill of Rights*. This policy offered compensation for a variety of departure delays and on-board ground delays. It even promised $1000 if, through overbooking, a customer were involuntarily bumped from a flight.

JetBlue Airways'
Customer Bill of Rights

Above all else, JetBlue Airways is dedicated to bringing humanity back to air travel. We strive to make every part of your experience as simple and as pleasant as possible. Unfortunately, there are times when things do not go as planned. If you're inconvenienced as a result, we think it is important that you know exactly what you can expect from us. That's why we created our Customer Bill of Rights. These Rights will always be subject to the highest level of safety and security for our customers and crewmembers.

INFORMATION
JetBlue will notify customers of the following:
- Delays prior to scheduled departure
- Cancellations and their cause
- Diversions and their cause

CANCELLATIONS
All customers whose flight is cancelled by JetBlue will, at the customer's option, receive a full refund or reaccommodation on the next available JetBlue flight at no additional charge or fare. If JetBlue cancels a flight within 4 hours of scheduled departure and the cancellation is due to a Controllable Irregularity, JetBlue will also issue the customer a $50 Voucher good for future travel on JetBlue.

DELAYS (Departure Delays or Onboard Ground Delays on Departure)
For customers whose flight is delayed 3 hours or more after scheduled departure, JetBlue will provide free movies on flights that are 2 hours or longer.

DEPARTURE DELAYS
1. Customers whose flight is delayed for 1-1:59 hours after scheduled departure time due to a *Controllable Irregularity* are entitled to a $25 Voucher good for future travel on JetBlue.
2. Customers whose flight is delayed for 2-4:59 hours after scheduled departure time due to a *Controllable Irregularity* are entitled to a $50 Voucher good for future travel on JetBlue.
3. Customers whose flight is delayed for 5-5:59 hours after scheduled departure time due to a *Controllable Irregularity* are entitled to a Voucher good for future travel on JetBlue in the amount paid by the customer for the oneway trip (or $50, whichever is greater).
4. Customers whose flight is delayed for 6 or more hours after scheduled departure time due to a *Controllable Irregularity* are entitled to a Voucher good for future travel on JetBlue in the amount paid by the customer for the roundtrip (or the oneway trip, doubled).

OVERBOOKINGS (As defined in JetBlue's Contract of Carriage)
Customers who are involuntarily denied boarding shall receive $1,000.

LAST UPDATED: 7/2008

ONBOARD GROUND DELAYS
JetBlue will provide customers experiencing an Onboard Ground Delay with 36 channels of DIRECTV®*, food and drink, access to clean restrooms and, as necessary, medical treatment. For customers who experience an Onboard Ground Delay for more than 5 hours, JetBlue will also take necessary action so that customers may deplane.

Arrivals:
1. Customers who experience an Onboard Ground Delay on Arrival for 1-1:59 hours after scheduled arrival time are entitled to a $50 Voucher good for future travel on JetBlue.
2. Customers who experience an Onboard Ground Delay on Arrival for 2 hours or more after scheduled arrival time are entitled to a Voucher good for future travel on JetBlue in the amount paid by the customer for the roundtrip (or the oneway trip, doubled).

Departures:
1. Customers who experience an Onboard Ground Delay on Departure after scheduled departure time for 3-3:59 hours are entitled to a $50 Voucher good for future travel on JetBlue.
2. Customers who experience an Onboard Ground Delay on Departure after scheduled departure time for 4-4:59 hours are entitled to a Voucher good for future travel on JetBlue in the amount paid by the customer for the oneway trip (or $50, whichever is greater).
3. Customers who experience an Onboard Ground Delay on Departure for 5 hours or more after scheduled arrival time are entitled to a Voucher good for future travel on JetBlue in the amount paid by the customer for the roundtrip (or the oneway trip, doubled).

In-flight entertainment:
JetBlue offers 36 channels of DIRECTV® service on its flights in the Continental U.S. If our LiveTV™ system is inoperable on flights in the Continental U.S., customers are entitled to a $15 Voucher good for future travel on JetBlue.

JetBlue Airways
118-29 Queens Blvd
Forest Hills, NY 11375

These Rights are subject to JetBlue's Contract of Carriage and, as applicable, the operational control of the flight crew, and apply to only JetBlue-operated flights.
*Available only on flights in the Continental U.S.

This document is representative of what is reflected in JetBlue's Contract of Carriage, the legally binding document between JetBlue and its customers, and its terms are incorporated herein.

Discussion questions

1

Define problem recognition in consumer decision making. Describe two different occasions when problem recognition may occur and provide examples of both.

2

Suppose you are on the market for a new computer. Describe the stages of the decision-making process that you would go through and what would occur at each stage as it relates to this purchase.

3

How does 'framing' impact consumer decision making?

4

There are two major heuristics used by consumers when they are engaged in low-effort decision making. Describe them and detail two instances when each heuristic could be used.

Exercise 1

Many interesting examples of framing effects can be found on the shelves of grocery stores. Make a visit to your local grocery store. Based on your understanding of the theory, locate an instance where the theory is being used appropriately and one where it is being used inappropriately.

Exercise 2

Identify four individuals who have made purchases in the past month with which they have been dissatisfied. How did each person respond? If any of them contacted the company or store where the purchase was made, how did the company respond? How would you advise the company to respond in the future?

Exercise 3

One strategy used in decision making occurs when consumers use country of origin as an anchor. Your task is to examine country-of-origin effect. Create a profile for a new laptop computer (you may alter a profile that already exists online). Increase the storage space and processor speed and decrease the weight in order to make the laptop more appealing to the consumer. At the beginning of the product description, add the line 'Made in x'. Create three descriptions where the only difference is the country where the product is made. Use three countries, one in South America, one in Western Europe and another in Asia. Ask three different individuals to rate the quality of each laptop. Assess the likelihood of their purchasing the laptop. Record their responses. Use one description per person. Did consumers respond differently to the laptop depending on its origin? What does this tell you about country-of-origin effects?

Endnotes

1
Gogoi, P. 'How Walmart's TV Prices Crushed Rivals' *Businessweek*, 23 April 2007

2
<www.gotmilk.com>

3
Johnson, E. J. and Russo, J. E. (1984) 'Product Familiarity and Learning New Information', *The Journal of Consumer Research*, Vol. 11, No. 1, pp. 542–550

4
Kahneman, D. and Tversky, A. 'On the Psychology of Prediction' *Psychology Review*, July 1973

5
Maheshwaran, D. 'Country of Origin as a Stereotype: Effects of consumer Expertise and Attribute Strengthen Product Evaluations' *Journal of Consumer Research*, September 1994

6
Tversky, A. and Kahneman, D. (1986) 'Rational choice and the framing of decision' *Journal of Business*

7
Tversky, A. and Kahneman, D. (1991) 'Loss Aversion in Riskless Choice: A Reference-Dependent Model', *The Quarterly Journal of Economics*

8
Payne, J. W., Bettman, J. R., and Johnson, E. J. (1992) 'Behavioural Decision Research: A Constructive Processing Perspective,' *Annual Review of Psychology*, Vol. 43, pp. 87–131

9
© 2001 Houghton Mifflin Company. All rights reserved

10
Bailey, J. 'JetBlue's C.E.O. Is "Mortified" After Fliers Are Stranded' *The New York Times*, 19 February 2007

Recommended reading

Why we Buy: The Science of Shopping
Paco Underhill
Simon & Schuster ■ 2008

Ostensibly, a business book aimed at merchandisers, *Why we Buy* also contains valuable information for consumers and students who want to understand the art of shopping and the science of selling.

Buyology: Truth and Lies About Why We Buy
Martin Lindstrom and Paco Underhill
Broadway Business ■ 2008

This book contains many interesting stories about how the brain and emotions drive consumer choice. The author uses recent functional Magnetic Resonance Imaging (fMRI) studies to shed light on the motivational forces that underlie consumer buying behaviour.

The 2007 Entertainment, Media & Advertising Market Research Handbook
Richard K. Miller
Richard K Miller & Associates ■ 2007

This paperback covers how consumers use their leisure time and details key players in the entertainment, media, and advertising industries, with profiles of major companies in each industry as well as rankings. There are also chapters on branding, including top brands; on direct marketing and outdoor advertising; sponsorships and licensing, entertainment marketing; on television and television advertising and programming; on film and video, radio, satellite and Internet radio, and print media; sports; and a series of chapters on the demographics of various markets.

International marketing data and statistics (annual)
Gale Group
Euromonitor Publications

Covers demographic trends and forecasts, economic indicators, labour force, trade, energy, environment, consumer expenditures and market size, and retailing information for the Americas, Asia, Africa and Oceania; companion volume to European marketing data and statistics.

European Marketing Data and Statistics (annual)
Euromonitor PLC
Euromonitor Publications

Again, covers demographic trends and forecasts, economic indicators, labour force, trade, energy, environment, consumer expenditures and market size, and retailing information but this time for European countries.

Best Customers: Demographics of Consumer Demand
New Strategist Publications Inc ■ 2008

Using data from the U.S. Bureau of Labor Statistics, this volume indicates who the best and biggest customers are for 300 specific products and services, with an analysis of household spending by age, income, race, region, etc.

The Blackwell Encyclopedic Dictionary of Marketing
Barbara R. Lewis and Dale Littler
Wiley-Blackwell ■ 2008

This paperback is arranged alphabetically by marketing topic, with short definitions of each topic (one to several paragraphs long). See pages 27 to 36 for Consumer Attitudes, Consumer Buyer Behaviour, Consumer Decision-Making Process, Consumer Learning, Consumer Marketing, and more.

Encyclopedia of Business Ethics and Society
Robert W. Kolb (Editor)
Sage Publications, Inc ■ 2007

This five-volume reference work includes 900 essays by
scholars, arranged alphabetically by topic, on all aspects
of business ethics. See entries for Consumer Fraud,
Consumer Goods, Consumer Preferences, and
Consumer Rights, in volume one.

Market Share Reporter: An Annual Compilation of Reported Market Share Data on Companies, Products, and Services
Robert S. Lazich (Editor)
Gacl

Annual two-volume compilation of market share data
on companies, products and services, both US and
international, arranged by SIC code and with indexes
by product, company and topic.

The IEBM Encyclopedia of Marketing (International Encyclopedia of Business & Management)
Michael J. Baker (Editor)
Thomson Learning ■ 2000

This volume includes 12-page essays on about 60 topics,
under such headings as marketing management, the
marketing mix, marketing in practice, and special topics.
See Consumer Behaviour on pp. 670 and 671.

Marketing Scales Handbook
Gordon C. Bruner, Paul J. Hensel, Karen E. James
South-Western Educational Pub ■ 2005

Volume three presents 941 scales culled from articles,
on marketing scales in consumer behaviour, published
in the top marketing journals between 1994 and 1997;
volume four provides all new or new uses of previously
developed scales in consumer behaviour and advertising
that appeared between 1998 and 2001, with 654 scales.
These volumes include two indexes, by author and
by publication.

Web resources

The Encyclopedia of Psychology
<www.psychology.org>

This online encyclopedia of psychology is maintained
by professors at an American University, with links to
academic articles on a wide variety of topics in this field.
The site covers the following topics:

- The biological factors underlying behaviour
- The study of psychological phenomena
- The history of psychology and its people
- Organizations and institutions of psychology
- Careers in psychology

The Consumer Psychologist's Newsletter
<www.consumerpsychologist.com>

This online newsletter features a concise discussion
of current events and issues in consumer marketing.
Newsletters contain words of wisdom and marketing
insight; they never exceed three pages in length.

The American Customer Satisfaction Index
<www.theacsi.org>

This organisation 'reports scores on a 0–100 scale at
the national level and produces indexes for 10 economic
sectors, 43 industries (including e-commerce and
e-business) and more than 200 companies and
federal or local government agencies. In addition to the
company-level satisfaction scores, ACSI produces scores
for the causes and consequences of customer satisfaction
and their relationships.'

Picture credits

Acknowledgments

Special thanks to Ann Middlebrook, and later
Georgia Kennedy, at AVA Publishing for their tireless work
in bringing this project to completion. I would not have
been in a position to pursue this project if it were not for
two major influences in my life. First, my family has been
there for me, continuously encouraging my academic
pursuits. This was in the form of my now deceased
father's drive for excellence in results, and my mother's
unwavering demand for excellence in effort. They have
both made me who I am today. Additionally, my goals
and commitment to success were further shaped by
my *alma mater,* Queen's Royal College, an institution
that creates well-rounded, socially adept scholars out
of exuberant young men. This august institution was
the perfect complement to my parents' insistence on
doing (and achieving) my best, even if someone else
'won the prize' – *Certant omnes, sed non omnibus palman.*

Dedication

This work is dedicated to my parents, Mona and Peter,
and my beautiful daughter, Annalise. You are always in
my thoughts and in my heart.

BASICS
MARKETING

Working with ethics

Lynne Elvins
Naomi Goulder

Publisher's note

The subject of ethics is not new, yet its consideration within the applied visual arts is perhaps not as prevalent as it might be. Our aim here is to help a new generation of students, educators and practitioners find a methodology for structuring their thoughts and reflections in this vital area.

AVA Publishing hopes that these **Working with ethics** pages provide a platform for consideration and a flexible method for incorporating ethical concerns in the work of educators, students and professionals. Our approach consists of four parts:

The **introduction** is intended to be an accessible snapshot of the ethical landscape, both in terms of historical development and current dominant themes.

The **framework** positions ethical consideration into four areas and poses questions about the practical implications that might occur. Marking your response to each of these questions on the scale shown will allow your reactions to be further explored by comparison.

The **case study** sets out a real project and then poses some ethical questions for further consideration. This is a focus point for a debate rather than a critical analysis so there are no predetermined right or wrong answers.

A selection of **further reading** for you to consider areas of particular interest in more detail.

Ethical: awareness/ reflection/ debate

Introduction

Ethics is a complex subject that interlaces the idea of responsibilities to society with a wide range of considerations relevant to the character and happiness of the individual. It concerns virtues of compassion, loyalty and strength, but also of confidence, imagination, humour and optimism. As introduced in ancient Greek philosophy, the fundamental ethical question is *what should I do?* How we might pursue a 'good' life not only raises moral concerns about the effects of our actions on others, but also personal concerns about our own integrity.

In modern times the most important and controversial questions in ethics have been the moral ones. With growing populations and improvements in mobility and communications, it is not surprising that considerations about how to structure our lives together on the planet should come to the forefront. For visual artists and communicators it should be no surprise that these considerations will enter into the creative process.

Some ethical considerations are already enshrined in government laws and regulations or in professional codes of conduct. For example, plagiarism and breaches of confidentiality can be punishable offences. Legislation in various nations makes it unlawful to exclude people with disabilities from accessing information or spaces. The trade of ivory as a material has been banned in many countries. In these cases, a clear line has been drawn under what is unacceptable.

But most ethical matters remain open to debate, among experts and lay-people alike, and in the end we have to make our own choices on the basis of our own guiding principles or values. Is it more ethical to work for a charity than for a commercial company? Is it unethical to create something that others find ugly or offensive?

Specific questions such as these may lead to other questions that are more abstract. For example, is it only effects on humans (and what they care about) that are important, or might effects on the natural world require attention too?

Is promoting ethical consequences justified even when it requires ethical sacrifices along the way? Must there be a single unifying theory of ethics (such as the Utilitarian thesis that the right course of action is always the one that leads to the greatest happiness of the greatest number), or might there always be many different ethical values that pull a person in various directions?

As we enter into ethical debate and engage with these dilemmas on a personal and professional level, we may change our views or change our view of others. The real test though is whether, as we reflect on these matters, we change the way we act as well as the way we think. Socrates, the 'father' of philosophy, proposed that people will naturally do 'good' if they know what is right. But this point might only lead us to yet another question: *how do we know what is right?*

You
What are your ethical beliefs?

Central to everything you do will be your attitude to people and issues around you. For some people their ethics are an active part of the decisions they make everyday as a consumer, a voter or a working professional. Others may think about ethics very little and yet this does not automatically make them unethical. Personal beliefs, lifestyle, politics, nationality, religion, gender, class or education can all influence your ethical viewpoint.

Using the scale, where would you place yourself? What do you take into account to make your decision? Compare results with your friends or colleagues.

Your client
What are your terms?

Working relationships are central to whether ethics can be embedded into a project and your conduct on a day-to-day basis is a demonstration of your professional ethics. The decision with the biggest impact is whom you choose to work with in the first place. Cigarette companies or arms traders are often-cited examples when talking about where a line might be drawn, but rarely are real situations so extreme. At what point might you turn down a project on ethical grounds and how much does the reality of having to earn a living effect your ability to choose?

Using the scale, where would you place a project? How does this compare to your personal ethical level?

01 02 03 04 05 06 07 08 09 10

01 02 03 04 05 06 07 08 09 10

Your specifications
What are the impacts of your materials?

In relatively recent times we are learning that many natural materials are in short supply. At the same time we are increasingly aware that some man-made materials can have harmful, long-term effects on people or the planet. How much do you know about the materials that you use? Do you know where they come from, how far they travel and under what conditions they are obtained? When your creation is no longer needed, will it be easy and safe to recycle? Will it disappear without a trace? Are these considerations the responsibility of you or are they out of your hands?

Using the scale, mark how ethical your material choices are.

Your creation
What is the purpose of your work?

Between you, your colleagues and an agreed brief, what will your creation achieve? What purpose will it have in society and will it make a positive contribution? Should your work result in more than commercial success or industry awards? Might your creation help save lives, educate, protect or inspire? Form and function are two established aspects of judging a creation, but there is little consensus on the obligations of visual artists and communicators toward society, or the role they might have in solving social or environmental problems. If you want recognition for being the creator, how responsible are you for what you create and where might that responsibility end?

Using the scale, mark how ethical the purpose of your work is.

01 02 03 04 05 06 07 08 09 10

01 02 03 04 05 06 07 08 09 10

One aspect of marketing that raises an ethical dilemma is the extent to which marketing techniques might persuade or influence consumers to purchase items that they may not need or that may even be detrimental. Central to this question is the balance of power in the relationship between the seller and the buyer. Marketers emphasise the positive attributes of a product or service and cement favourable associations in the minds of the target audience, usually to generate sales. In free markets, buyers should be able to compare and choose from a variety of competitive options. However, as marketing has become increasingly diverse in its formats and complex in its application of psychological techniques, questions can be raised about the freedom of individuals to choose fairly. Do marketers genuinely feel positive about the products and services that they help to promote, or are they driven purely to make profit for themselves and the seller? Should marketing people have responsibility for ensuring that buyers can make fully informed choices? Or is this issue already taken care of through independent consumer groups and anti-trust law?

In the mid-1980s, the social marketing of condoms emerged as an effective tool in the fight to combat the spread of HIV/AIDS. Programmes made condoms available, affordable and acceptable in countries affected by the epidemic, particularly in sub-Saharan Africa, and used marketing messages to raise awareness of the disease.

Complex cultural factors can present a challenge for HIV prevention, education and condom promotion. For example, due to gender inequalities, young girls and women are regularly and repeatedly denied information about, and access to, condoms. Therefore, condoms must be marketed in ways that help to overcome sexual and personal obstacles to their use.

One marketing technique that might be deployed is to recruit prominent individuals and groups to deliver and endorse safer sex messages. This approach has been successful through the recruitment of sports and music figures, religious leaders and politicians. In 1996, Archbishop Tutu delivered an impassioned plea for South Africans to face the facts about HIV and AIDS in a television documentary entitled 'The Rubber Revolution'. Tutu, along with Catholic and Muslim leaders and various national sports figures, discussed the importance of open conversations about sexuality and HIV/AIDS. Prior to Tutu's involvement, the South African Broadcasting Corporation had not allowed the word 'condom' to be used on primetime television.

The Society for Family Health (SFH) in Nigeria also launched a high-profile marketing campaign using former world-class football star, Sunday Oliseh, who is a prominent role model in Nigeria. SFH produced print, radio and television messages with Oliseh promoting Gold Circle, a specially created brand of condom, along with condom use and the practice of safer sex. The campaign was launched simultaneously with the 1998 World Cup Soccer tournament, in which Oliseh led the national team.

With support from USAID and other non-profit organisations, the condom brand Prudence was introduced to Zaire in 1996. Previous to this campaign, the total number of condoms given away or sold in Zaire was approximately 500,000 a year. In 1999, four million Prudence condoms were sold. A key tactic in the marketing campaign was the placement and pricing strategy. By selling Prudence condoms via street hawkers at three cents each, people were able to get hold of condoms anywhere at any time. Salespeople were also supported with Prudence key rings, bartender aprons, calendars, hats and signs; and music events offered half-price admission to anyone with a Prudence pack. The marketing campaign has been so successful that Zairians now use 'Prudence' as a generic term for a condom.

Is it more ethical to practice social marketing than purely commercial marketing?

Is it unethical to pay somebody to endorse a product or service that they may not otherwise use?

Would you work on a project to market condoms in African countries?

There is an increasing political and social consensus that something needs to be done to safeguard children from the worst excesses of direct marketing and the pressures of commercialisation.

Reverend Dr Rowan Williams, the Archbishop of Canterbury <www.christiantoday.com>

AIGA
Design business and ethics
2007, AIGA

Eaton, Marcia Muelder
Aesthetics and the good life
1989, Associated University Press

Ellison, David
Ethics and aesthetics in European modernist literature
2001, Cambridge University Press

Fenner, David EW (Ed.)
Ethics and the arts: an anthology
1995, Garland Reference Library of Social Science

Gini, Al (Ed.)
Case studies in business ethics
2005, Prentice Hall

McDonough, William and Braungart, Michael
'Cradle to Cradle: Remaking the Way We Make Things'
2002

Papanek, Victor
'Design for the Real World: Making to Measure'
1971

United Nations
Global Compact the Ten Principles www.unglobalcompact.org/
AboutTheGC/TheTenPrinciples/index.html